Swallowed
By A Snake

The Gift of the
Masculine Side of Healing

NOTE TO USERS

This information is considered by B.C. Cancer Agency staff to offer clear, general information concerning cancer care which will help to answer frequently asked questions. However, in some instances, it may contain treatment or related information which varies from Agency practice.

This material is not intended to replace advice given by your physician or other health care providers. If you have any questions or would like more current information or further guidance, you are encouraged to speak to your cancer specialist, other Clinic staff or your personal physician.

Swallowed
By A Snake

The Gift of the
Masculine Side of Healing

Second Edition

Thomas R. Golden, LCSW

Golden Healing Publishing L.L.C.
149 Little Quarry Mews
Gaithersburg, Maryland 20878

Copyright 1996, 2000 Golden Healing Publishing, L.L.C.
Library of Congress Control Number: 00-092176
ISBN: 0-9654649-1-1

In honor of my father,
Thomas S. Golden

Contents

The Ground of the Battle

Preface to the Second Edition

The response to *Swallowed by a Snake: The Gift of the Masculine Side of Healing* has been amazing and gratifying. Both men and women have used this book in their healing process, and many have shared their grief experiences with me. In this light, the second edition of *Swallowed by a Snake* includes an Epilogue describing my own grief process.

The essays comprising the Epilogue were written following the death of my father. They trace my own healing through individual, communal, and family rituals and actions that helped me to express and heal my grief. They follow the path of my healing, from delivering the funeral eulogy through planting a tree in his honor and designing a family commemoration on the anniversary of his death to finally watching the tide of my grief begin to recede.

I offer these essays as a window into one man's experience of grief, and an example of how the concepts and suggestions of this book can be translated into concrete actions of healing. I hope you will find my experience beneficial in your own journey toward healing.

Tom Golden
July 2000

Introduction

Swallowed by a Snake is a book that both men and women will find helpful. A man reading these pages will find a book that honors the uniqueness of a man's path toward healing. A woman reading this book will benefit not only from gaining a deeper understanding of the men in her life, she will find herself in these pages. Although the majority of examples are about men it is an indisputable fact that women find this masculine gift a powerful ally in their own path toward healing. Both genders have access to the gift of the masculine side of healing. Each of us has both masculine and feminine qualities—it is our unique blend of these that determines our best path to healing.

The masculine side of healing is not as accepted a mode of healing as the more traditional verbal and emotional expressions. It tends to be quieter and less visible, less connected with the past and more connected with the future; less connected with passivity and more aligned with action. As a consequence, I have noticed repeatedly that people who use a predominance of this masculine side of healing are suspected even by mental health professionals of "not really healing."

As a beginning grief therapist in the late 1970's I can remember the difference I felt when a new client I would receive was a man or a woman. Somehow a woman seemed easier to work with, requiring less effort in helping her to do her work. A man, on the other hand, many times meant trouble. Somehow men didn't seem to fit our program. Being the only male therapist, I would tend to get most of the male referrals. The reaction of the female therapists to male clients was somewhat stronger than my own, with some staff members even refusing to work with men. Various criticisms were heard about the way men grieved or didn't grieve. It took me some time to realize that the type of therapy I had been taught to do was designed for women. The vast majority of clients who visit therapists' offices are female, and due to this, therapy is shaped accordingly to fit and be effective with women. I slowly began to realize that there wasn't something wrong with the men—there was something wrong with the therapy. This book will take you on a journey that parallels my own struggle in finding out what does and doesn't help men in healing their grief.

Swallowed by a Snake is divided into three sections. The first section begins with three chapters devoted to understanding the experience of being swallowed by the snake. What is it? What makes it difficult? How do we get out of it? Through my years of experience in working with men and grief I have found that men need grief defined in this different manner. Chapter one will begin by defining grief in terms that men will understand. Terms like chaos and desire will supplant the usual definitions of grief in terms of feelings. The second chapter will give information to assist people in gauging their grief. It will explain the reasons why some kinds of grief are more difficult to handle than others.   The third chapter provides a practical guide to the mechanics of ritual in order to allow each person to evaluate and understand their own way of healing.

Section two is comprised of four chapters and examines more closely the experience of healing through the masculine gift. In chapter four we begin with a story that illustrates the importance of standing in the tension of your grief. By this I mean consciously and willingly experiencing your pain. We then look into what facilitates a man's connection to his grief, and what makes this connection difficult.

In chapter five we focus on the building blocks of grief: the experience of feelings. We take four of the feelings of grief—anger, sadness, helplessness, and guilt—and discuss how they relate to a man's grief and how each one is difficult or not for a man to process. These are certainly not the totality of feelings in any grief response, but in my experience these four emotions accompany the vast majority of grief reactions.

In chapter six we will look into some of the reasons behind gender differences in processing feelings, and specifically in grieving. Men and women have different paths in processing and healing their grief, and this chapter will examine the underlying reasons for these differences.

In chapter seven we examine "different" ways to grieve. These ways are different because they vary from the traditional healing of grief through crying and talking about it. We will give examples of these different ways, showing how men have connected their pain and tears to ritual activities. These actions are divided into three categories: creativity, practicality, and thinking. All of these categories can include actions, places, or things which aid men or women in connecting with their grief.

It is important to note that the gift of the masculine side of healing (usually action-oriented) is not exclusive to men; many women use these modes of healing and use them well. In the same vein, many men use relational skills (crying and talking about it) to heal their grief. We are painting with broad strokes if we attempt to link men with action and women with relating. In general, men tend toward action as a primary mode in healing their grief while using relating as secondary, and women are the opposite. What we are describing are tendencies, not hard and fast rules about a man's way versus a woman's way. Perhaps a helpful way to look at it is that men have a feminine side and women have a masculine side, and it depends on your own unique mix of these two as to how you will choose to process your grief. As you are reading, you might want to frame it in such a way that when we are speaking of men, you think of your own masculine qualities and when we speak of women, you are reminded of your feminine side.

The last section focuses on the "ground" on which we struggle to heal ourselves— our culture and its lack of a socially-sanctioned ritual process. This lack makes grieving difficult for both men and women. In chapter eight we will look at examples of the way people have grieved over the last thousand years in order to bring some contrast and understanding to our present state of ritual poverty. We will see that our culture is deficient in sanctioned rituals for healing grief.

Chapter nine will show how indigenous cultures around the world have made grief a part of their lives and honored the difference in healing paths of men and women. We will see how these cultures have honored men's and women's unique needs in healing their grief. The two cultures which are featured will show men and women performing rituals together, functioning as a team, but playing their own unique roles within the process. From this we can draw ideas and insight to aid us in our own healing, and in our understanding of how men and women can work together in a healing effort.

Grief is a problem without an easy solution. When anyone confronts a problem that has no solution he or she will often feel lost. When a woman feels lost, she tends to ask for help. When a man feels lost, he looks for a map. This book is intended to be that map. I hope you find this material helpful.

1
What Is Grief?

Grief is the garden of the heart.
Rumi

Grief is a part of life. We are familiar with our responses to gain and celebration, and grief is the other side of that coin. Grief, simply put, is the physical, emotional, and mental responses we have to a loss of any kind. We expect grief to flow from a major loss such as the death of a friend or family member, but it can also flow in smaller amounts from ordinary, everyday losses. Such losses might be the conclusion of your favorite time of year, a holiday, or being in a traffic jam and late for an important meeting. These smaller losses are examples of what is termed micro-grief. Grief can be related to losses of childhood, such as the loss of seeing the world as a safe place, or all of the unmet expectations, thwarted intentions, or unspoken communications we might have stored inside us. When looked at in this way, we begin to see that grief is an integral part of being alive, a part of our daily living. It is woven into the fabric of life.

Grief and Desire

Grief is related to desire. Desire is the source of both grief and happiness; if you have desires of any kind you will undoubtedly have grief. If your desire is met, you may find joy, and if it isn't, there is grief. Joy and grief are brothers in a way, and if you experience one fully you will probably experience the other in its fullness. If you deny either one, you will limit the other to the same degree. If you deny your grief, you limit your joy; if you deny your joy, you limit your grief.

A man I worked with named Phil immediately saw how this related to his own life. He said, "You know, that's why I had all those upsetting feelings at my mid-life period. I was dealing with all my unmet desires for success at work." He remembered his fantasies of huge success, at being top in his field, and realized that when he reached mid-life he experienced the loss of the possibility of his dreams coming to fruition.

Everything is Temporary

Even when some desires are met, however, the feelings of joy and fulfillment don't last forever. As the desire is met, we have a temporary state of happiness, but loss soon follows. We have lost the experience of the satisfaction of our desire and now it is gone, leaving us in a state of loss, wishing for the desire to be re-gratified. A typical example in our culture is the loss associated with weekends. If you look forward to your weekend and anticipate its arrival, there is probably desire associated with it. As the weekend closes on Sunday evening what is your reaction? The desired events have now been finished. This is most likely a very small loss, but our reactions to it can give us clues about how we grieve. Do you get irritable and edgy on Sunday evening? Do you try to squeeze in all of the joys you feel were left out? What mood underlies this effort? Do you experience anger or sadness?

From Micro-Grief to Major Grief

The way we respond to very small losses is many times similar to the way we will handle big losses. Our response could be sadness, anger, helplessness, or many others. When a person we love dies, we are flooded with a torrent of unmet desire. We have strong desires to have that person with us still. There are desires to re-experience some of the positive ways we may have connected with that person in the past. We have a variety of unmet desires relating to the person who died. This is the more familiar form of grief, but it differs from micro-grief only in its intensity and duration.

There is no recipe that can predict a person's emotional response to their lost desire. It is a very personal and individual response. Some people have thought that grief followed a specific and linear path, that grief had well defined, additive stages. These ideas have pretty much gone by the wayside. We have come to realize that the so-called five stages—denial, anger, sadness, bargaining, and acceptance—are really only experiences that have no particular order, except that denial is almost always first. Most people think of denial as something to be avoided, that it is somehow bad. What they don't realize is that denial works in both directions; it filters out the excessively wonderful things that happen to us as surely as it filters out the trauma. The first thing a lottery winner says is "I can't believe it." Denial acts as a shock absorber for our ego for both the good and the bad. In a computer, when data are changed the effect is immediate. But our brains and egos are not binary like a computer. It is as if our brains are "wetware," not hardware. In our situation the data change is not immediate, and denial spares us the jolting nature of receiving an extreme message.

In working with people who are grieving I have noticed that many people can go through all of the "five stages" in a single day. A man named Jeff came to me due to the death of his sister and mother. The deaths were fairly recent, and Jeff described a day in which he found himself first denying that the deaths had occurred, then a short time later remembering the truth of the loss. He next found himself angry and sad, and shortly thereafter, felt a more accepting attitude toward the deaths. It is not uncommon to cycle through many different responses in a short period of time. This doesn't mean that Jeff had resolved the loss; it is a normal part of grief to zoom up and down with feelings.

Reactions to Grief

There are numerous other reactions in grief, including getting in touch with the loss, holding on, letting go, making new attachments, and observing one's growth through the loss, etc. Getting in touch with the loss is just as it sounds. It is the reaction that most people equate with grief, usually characterized as being "in" the feelings. Holding on is a sense of not wanting to release the desires of the past and steadfastly holding on to them. Letting go is a time when we are ready to release the desires. Making new attachments is the process where we begin to feel our desires growing again, and we feel strong enough to begin to make other attachments. All of these different reactions can manifest at any time. You can even have denial near the end of a grief, just as you can have resolutions of parts of the grief in the very beginning.

Grief and Depression

What is the difference between grief and depression? I like to think of them as being very different processes. Grief is our unique and natural response to loss, while depression is many times a web of negative self-thoughts. When we are depressed, we are in some way thinking that we are a terrible person. The thoughts can range from "I could never do that" to "I have committed the unpardonable sin." Depression is a deflated state of mind that we tend to act out. By this, I mean that our behavior will follow our thoughts. If we think that we are the worst schlub in the world, then our actions will often follow suit. Grief, on the other hand, is the ability to "stand in our own tension" arising from a loss. It is the natural response to a normal life experience. Many times when a depressed person begins to feel what is inside—not the negative thought processes but the feelings within—they are starting to heal themselves. The distinction can get a bit complicated, but the general rule is that grief is related to the acknowledgment, honoring, and often expression of feeling connected to a loss, and depression is a form of pathological negative thinking.

Grief is like a Beast

Grief can be likened to a beast: it comes in many shapes and sizes. Micro-grief might look like a small beast, a bird or an insect perhaps, in keeping with a loss related to a small desire of some sort. Then there are larger varieties that could be likened to dragons. Their size is unreal to us, and they are so powerful that they appear to be from another world. It is this dragon type of grief that is related to Joseph Campbell's idea of the "call." Campbell related the world's great mythologies as a metaphor for times in our life when we were "called" to leave our everyday existence and enter a new landscape teeming with danger. As we experience such a grief, we are drawn out of our normal functioning and thrust into a world and a part of ourselves that is very unfamiliar terrain. The grief has become the dragon of myth, and we are faced with what Campbell has called the hero's journey. By approaching and confronting this dragon we open ourselves to an inner quest that has all of the trappings of a distant land—danger and unknown landscapes. We can choose not to fight the dragon, but if we do so there is certainly a price for that. The price is that we always have a dragon on our heels, breathing fire down our necks. We find ourselves unable to engage in life, and always having to look over our shoulder to check on the dragon.

An example of this is a man named Joe. Joe experienced the traumatic death of his wife when he was 34 years old, but chose not to fight the dragon. When he came into therapy at the age of 44, he was exhausted from ten years of evading the dragon. He had made a conscious choice to not grieve the death of his wife. His decision was related to a variety of factors, one of which was that he wanted to maintain an image of being on top of things. Another factor was that he had a great deal of unfinished business from his childhood, old dragons. These old dragons took many forms, but the biggest one was his pain related to being physically abused by his father. Joe knew that if he fought this dragon (his wife's death), the other dragons, including the memories and pain related to his abuse, would come out. During that ten years Joe's life had been a "plain vanilla" existence, his energy and zest for living diminished by the dragons. His experience of life was that of drudgery, day in and day out just going through the motions of life, with very little feeling, either positive or negative. As Joe began to confront this dragon, the older ones did come out. Much to his surprise, he was able to slowly handle his inner dragons, and with time he regained his engagement with his own life. Turning away from dragons is a dangerous habit that can arise in many ways, as illustrated by the thousands of people who were abused as children and have never found a way to fight their dragons.

Inner Experience

What is the inner experience like when we confront our dragon? The feelings we experience when we meet a dragon are not of the ordinary variety. They are powerful and all consuming—anger, sadness, helplessness, fear, guilt, loneliness. A man I know was experiencing such feelings after the death of his father. He was surprised at the intensity of the feelings and started to discuss this with some of his closest friends. They advised him to "let it go," don't hold on to those feelings. The man was hurt by their advice, knowing that it was off the mark. His friends had no conception of what he was going through. His own assessment of the situation was that his experience was very much like treading water, trying to keep his head above the surface. "How can I let go of something I'm swimming in?" he asked. This is the way it is when we meet a grief that is like a dragon.

Grief and the Body

There are experiences of dragon grief other than feelings. One example is what happens to the body. Common complaints include fatigue and inability to sleep well. A man named John experienced fatigue so intense that he could barely get out of bed in the morning. It was a struggle to do anything, his energy level was so low. This was amplified by a change in his sleeping habits. At one point in his grief he found himself waking up at night and not being able to get back to sleep. During this time of wakefulness he was besieged by feelings. The body also reacts to the fight by giving us signals, registering sensations that are symbols of the conflict that is ensuing.

These signals can be helpful markers for men in working with their grief. Often it is easier for a man to connect with his grief through his sensations in his body rather than making a connection through talking or thinking about it. Grief also affects our cognitive state. Many men report a decline in capacity to concentrate and a loss of short term memory. Others frequently experience their lowest levels of self esteem while in the midst of grief.

Any person's experience of grief is unique to them. There is no rule that says you will always experience this or that. You may experience any of the above possibilities or you may experience grief completely differently. You need to observe your grief and see how you react individually. Everyone is different, and the important thing is to observe and understand your own grief.

Swallowed by a Snake

The following story may help in looking at other aspects of grief:

Long, long ago, in a place far south of here, there was a village at the edge of the jungle. This village was a peaceable place except for one major problem, the boa constrictor. These boas were not the snakes we know today; they were huge snakes many times as large as the boas of our modern world. They were uncontrolled animals whose viciousness was only exceeded by their appetite. Much of the time they ate other animals, but without a doubt the boas' favorite dish was humans. Snakes would enter the village at will and eat whatever and whomever they pleased. There was no place to hide from these monstrous beasts.

One day in the village, a woman was speaking openly about her pain related to the boa. She spoke of her two children who had been devoured by this beast and was lamenting the state of affairs of having to live in such an unsafe place. She wondered aloud if there might not be someone who could put this snake reign of terror to an end. Her hope was that the men, women, and children of the village could live in peace.

A man had been listening to her pain and suffering. He was the man who played the flute most beautifully. He pondered her words and knew that something must be done. He packed his bundle of maize and his small knife, and off he went into the jungle, playing his flute as he walked.

The man carefully chose his spot in the jungle and sat and played his flute. He was aware that the boa was approaching, but continued his playing. Then without warning the snake attacked and swallowed the flute player with one bite. The darkness from within the snake's belly was complete. The flute player tried to make himself as comfortable as possible, then unpacked his belongings and took out his knife. He consciously and deliberately used the knife to cut away the snake's belly a bit at a time. The snake reacted to this tremendous pain in its belly by making as much room for the flute player as it possibly could.

The flute player knew that it was going to take awhile to complete the task of killing this huge snake. He proceeded to cut and eat a bit of the snake's flesh each time he got hungry. This went on for quite some time, and the snake was continually in pain. He made it a point to tell all of his snake friends to never again eat a human, or they would suffer the consequences of this great pain that he now felt.

After awhile the flute player came to the boa's heart. Upon cutting this, the boa died. At that point the flute player emerged from the snake and returned to the village playing his flute. Everyone in the village was surprised to see him and asked where he had been. The flute player responded that he had been in the boa, and to prove it he showed them a piece of the snake's heart. The people then knew that the snake was indeed dead.[1]

This beautiful story speaks about grief. It tells us that going into grief may at times be like being eaten by a snake. We are cut off from our everyday life, we feel that our existence is confined, and we are surrounded by our grief like the flute player was. Our world is completely changed, going from life as we know it into the belly of a snake. Imagine being in the belly of a huge snake. Dark. A very tight spot. Every place you turn, there is the belly of the snake. The entire environment is this wet, warm, restrictive belly, pulling at you to conform to its wishes. This is similar to the way a person may feel who is experiencing a deep grief. Sometimes the grief takes over, and you feel that your life has to conform to the grief rather than to your own wishes.

Being in the Belly

Many times we have a sense that there is no way out of the situation, that the grief we are experiencing is never going to end. Part of a significant grief is the feeling that the grief has become the only reality and will continue forever. The flute player must have sometimes felt the same as he experienced his struggle. He took his bag of maize and knife with him, realizing that this was not a short term project. He knew that he must cut away a little bit of the belly at a time, and he seemed to have faith that eventually he would get to the "heart of the matter." This is the way it is with grief. We need to come prepared and be ready for the long haul. Grief is not a short term project; some types are lifelong struggles. With the death of a child for example, the parents are in the belly of grief for years. After the first year or two they find that they are still in the belly. Although probably not in the same way as they experienced it in the first year after the death, the pain is still strong and stays strong for a long time. This kind of loss leaves behind the old metaphor for grief which is that of a wound, and brings forth a different image: that of an amputation. Dealing with a loss like the death of a child is more like learning how to live after a part of you has been cut off than it is like healing from a wound. What I have seen these people do is to find other parents who are also in the belly and form small communities that can honor their grief. Our culture superficially expects that these parents will heal from their grief in a relatively short period of time, and it just is not so. Often I have worked with a parent who has been asked by a friend, "Aren't you over that yet?" Sometimes this question comes after only a few months. We need to honor these people for learning how to live in the belly and not tacitly demand that they don't mention the belly they are in.

The flute player was prepared for his journey. He took along what he would need for his prolonged struggle. He didn't kill the snake with one blow; he knew that he had to carve away a bit at a time. This is the way it is with grief; we need to carve away at it a bit at a time. We need to realize that each time we experience the emotions involved in our grief we are taking another chunk out of the snake's belly and getting a little closer to the heart of the matter. Many times people don't realize that this is the nature of grief. They feel that honoring and acknowledging their grief is not having any effect. The snake wants you to feel that it is hopeless, that you are never getting out, that your pain is endless, that you should lie down and be digested. This is not the case. With most grief, cutting away a bit at a time will eventually lead you out of the belly.

In our story, one of the reasons the flute player responded to the call of the village woman was that children were being killed. This is also true with grief. When we are carrying unresolved grief within us and dragging the snake behind us, we lose our child-like qualities, such as spontaneity and creativity. Our child within is being strangled. Our reasons for wanting to kill the snake should include the renewal of our passion and creativity, which will emerge after we leave the snake.

When in the belly, we must learn a different way of living. In this dark, restrictive environment our usual skills for living are not particularly effective. The situation calls on us to use parts of ourselves that are not our usual strengths. Instead of seeing clearly what is before us, we might have to grope around, using our sense of touch rather than our eyes. Once our activity has brought us into the belly, we may need to find or develop other skills that will help us in navigating this inner terrain.

The flute player in our story found a way to enter his grief through his flute playing. The masculine gift tends to find activities that will help us in being in the belly, and this is the case with many men in our culture. With our void of socially-endorsed grieving rituals, men have had to be creative in finding active ways to lead them into their boa. Many times the activities that men find, like our protagonist's flute playing, will be related to their psychological strengths. Finding and using this strength as a means to enter into grief is a vital exercise for men and women. Notice that the flute player did not continue playing once he was in the belly; he had to use other skills in order to deal with the snake. Also notice that his work was not done from the outside, but was accomplished from inside the snake. This is the way it is with grief. We must do this work from the inside, but find our way into it through our strengths.

2
How To Gauge Your Grief

In the following pages we will have a look at the most important variables that affect the intensity and duration of grief. After reading this chapter you will have the tools to evaluate any loss you might experience and be able to make a rough prediction about the strength of the grief that will follow. These are the same variables that a good grief therapist would use in helping anyone evaluate his or her grief. This information will assist you in taking responsibility for your own grieving process.

Attachment

What makes one loss more difficult to handle than another? There are a number of variables involved, one being the amount of attachment to the object that is lost. You can see this in your own reactions to people you have known who have died. The more attached you are to that person, the greater will be the grief. Accordingly, we would expect that a person would be more "attached" to a parent than to a distant uncle. Attachment has to do with the connectedness one has with that person or object. A man might be more attached to an automobile than to a hammer, for instance. Many times we men become quite attached to our cars. When it comes time to sell it, a bit of grief might accompany the transaction, even though we might be purchasing a new and better car.

I once worked with a musician who cut his hand while assisting at the scene of a car accident. This injury put him out of work, unable to play his keyboard. There was even the chance that he might never regain his former playing capacity. The accident put the man into a state of crisis, and grief was one component of that crisis. For most of us such an injury would have been a small nuisance or inconvenience, but for this man it was a career- threatening experience. He was understandably attached to the precise and practiced movements of his hand. Because of the intensity of his attachment, his grief was more profound.

Expectedness

Another variable is that of expectedness. Is the loss expected? As our car grows older and becomes more of a burden and a problem, we prepare ourselves for its demise. We expect that it will be traded in. This expectation is what the experts call anticipatory grief, the acknowledgment of the loss prior to the event of the loss. As the car becomes older, we let go of our attachment by grieving the loss prior to the event. We might say, "I love that car, but it is getting older and I have got to do something about it." The seeds of grief are within our statement. "I love that car" is speaking to the attachment and "it is getting older and I have to do something about it" is speaking to the expectation of loss. We are acknowledging the connection to the object and the expected loss.

The same principle works with dying people. How expected is the loss? The grief from a death of someone who was in a boating accident that happened completely unexpectedly is significantly different than the grief from a death resulting from a long involved illness. During that long illness the griever has the opportunity to finish his emotional business with the dying person. This might include rehashing their times together, speaking of how that person will be remembered, or what will be missed about the person. Many times men will find something to do for the person who is dying in order to show their connection and love for that person. I remember a client I was working with who was dying of cancer. He was an older man who had gotten a great deal of joy from tending his vegetable garden. As this man became more ill, limiting his mobility, I started visiting him in his home. One day I asked him about his garden, and he looked out the window and sighed, "It looks pretty awful." That day after we had finished talking I went out and weeded the plot of land that had been so important to him. Although we never talked much about it, I think we both knew that this was my way of telling him how much I cared for him.

This process of concluding our business, whether through talking or doing something, is a cornerstone to grief work. It is a framework within which the feelings that exist are honored and acknowledged. It is considerably easier to accomplish when the person is alive. When you have a friend or relative who is dying, using the time in this manner is doing the work of grief. When you sit with that person and reminisce about old times and what you have done together, that is the work of grief. When you tell that person how they have affected your life, how they will be remembered, or how they are important to you, that is the work of grief. All of these things are acknowledging and honoring your attachment, and when we do that it is the work of grief. These activities help in bringing closure to our relationship with the dying person. I want to mention that honoring negative attachments is also a part of grief work, maybe even of more relative importance than the positive. Anticipatory grief is a process that means completing your business, both good and bad. Would you finish a business deal without letting the person know that there were some things that you didn't like about the work that you did together? Probably not. In the same way when we are grieving we need to include both the negative and the positive.

Naturalness

Is the loss natural? In the example of the car, it seemed natural for the car to be traded in; it had served its useful purpose, and it seemed right for it to be let go. Compare this with how you might feel if your car were wrecked unexpectedly. The more natural the loss the easier it will be to grieve. For instance, is the death you are facing that of a person who is 96 years old or that of a child who is three? The death of the older person seems more natural to us. The death of the child seems unnatural, and out of the order of our universe.

I once worked with a man whose teenage son had died suddenly. The man was returning home from shopping for a new car as a graduation gift for his son when he noticed a car accident. He stopped to help and realized that one of the cars was his son's. He ran to the car and found his son slumped over the steering wheel. After being helicoptered to the hospital, his son died. The man had no time to prepare for this great loss because he had no reason to expect that his son might die. This lack of preparation makes the loss more difficult to grieve. This death also seems unnatural. For a child to die seems to break the order of the universe. There is a Bhuddist prayer of blessing that begins something like this: "May you die, then your son die, then his son die, then his son die......"

Reportedly, the king for whom it was written was at first enraged by the prayer. It took the monk who wrote it some time to convey its true meaning—that the blessing is the generations dying in the "proper" order. When events don't follow their proper order there is usually increased grief.

Ambivalence

Ambivalence is related to our grief response. The general rule is that the more ambivalence, the more difficult the loss will be to grieve. For instance, if you have only love towards an object or person, the grieving process will be easier than if you have both love and hate. If you have all hate towards an object or person, then you will also have an easier time in grieving. Rarely do we have all hate or love for anyone or anything. Most often we have a big gray area that has some of each. When we have a great deal of love and a great deal of hate, that is great ambivalence. The greater the ambivalence the more difficult will be the grieving.

We almost always have some ambivalence for our parents. Imagine that as a child you couldn't get your father to watch you do things. Every time you jumped from the couch to the living room floor and flew for those few seconds, you preceded the flight with "Dad, watch." Unfortunately he rarely did. He was too absorbed in the newspaper or a phone conversation, or was not there at all. Each time you flew and were not watched there was grief. Robert Moore talks of the eyes of the king and how important they are. People want to be seen and be blessed by the king. They want to have an audience with the royal person, and in doing so, have their own life and worth honored and blessed. This same dynamic goes on in families. The royal persons are the mother and father, and if they will bless us by their watching and encouraging, then our small efforts are honored and seem somehow more worthwhile. When they don't watch us there is grief. We are attached to the idea that we want to be watched, and when we are not, instead of a blessing, there is a curse. We expect that they will watch us, we keep trying over and over to get them to watch us, and at some point we may even give up. We begin to think it is fruitless to get the king to watch, that he is not interested in our development. To us, it seems unnatural for the king not to watch.   The obvious truth to this matter is that no parent is able to watch each time the child desires. Therefore, with even the best of environments, we all experience this kind of loss in our upbringing. When this happens, grief and ambivalence are accumulated.

Dependency

Another variable is that of dependency. How dependent are we on the person who died, or the object that was lost? The greater the dependency the more prolonged and difficult the grief. A man I knew named John was married to a woman who was on a fast track in her career as an advertising executive. She made enough money that John had the option to cut back on his own work and spend more time with their children. He chose to work three days a week and spend the other two days at home with their two young children. John came to enjoy greatly his time with the kids. Then one day he got word that his wife had been killed in a car accident. A part of this great loss for John was related to his dependency on his wife for financial security. Men can develop various dependencies on their spouses. Examples might be dependence for social activities, emotional support, sexuality, or household management. Any time there is dependence on the person who dies it has an amplifying effect on one's grief.

A humorous example of this is the widower who has been dependent on his wife for years for doing the laundry. Among older widowers there is a common story. These men usually chuckle as they describe calling the appliance repairman to fix their dryer. The men get a surprise as the repairman tells them that all they have to do is to close the dryer door. Older widowed women, on the other hand, have their stories about going to the gas station and being completely perplexed about how to pump the gas. These are small examples of minor dependencies, but even the small dependencies have some effect on the grief. The bigger the dependency, the more difficulty is caused with the grief.

Grief Accumulates

Many of us know about anger and how if we don't acknowledge it and express it we will eventually explode or implode. Grief is the same way—it has a cumulative nature. The more grief we accumulate, the more powerful is the pressure inside. A metaphor for this might be the process of paying our bills. Most of us have a place to put unpaid bills. Imagine that you had a couple of bills on the counter or wherever you might put them. During your work day you don't consciously think of these unpaid bills, but there is some effect of having them there. It is as if they are quietly asking to be paid. There is a quiet voice that says "pay me," and until we do, the voice persists. Now imagine that there were lots of bills on the counter. What would the reaction be? Most of us would feel a heavier responsibility, a louder voice, or a more nagging sensation of needing to pay those bills. When we did finally pay them, what would the feeling be? It might be one of relief, and a greater capacity to enjoy the present moment. Grief is the same way. The more accumulation we have, the more we will have an urge to finish off this old stuff. Within our culture however, sometimes the more grief we accumulate, the more numb we will become to attempt to avoid paying the debt.

Letting Go and Holding On

What keeps us from paying this debt? There is a lot written these days about "letting go" of grief. This letting go is all well and good, but for many of us, men in particular, we don't know what it is we need to let go of. The whole idea of letting go needs to be prefaced by understanding that before we let go of anything, we must first "hold on" to it. It is this holding on that I have found is the most difficult thing for men to begin to do. We often have a hard time finding the inner state of loss. It seems vague and nebulous, less real than today's work at the office. It seems distant and not a part of being alive right now. Men who have recently gotten in touch with their grief express their surprise at how they feel a sense of relief along with the pain they experience. This relief is connected to the beginnings of paying off our unfinished grief.

The variables of attachment, expectedness, naturalness, dependency, and ambivalence can give us some ideas about the path and power our grief will take. An example of how these might work together could be a man who was laid off from work. The more he expected the layoff, the more time he will have to absorb the loss and prepare in some way for his future. If he has little time to prepare for this loss, he will be more shocked by the event and his grief will tend to be extended accordingly. The more he was attached to his job, the more he will tend to grieve for it's loss. Men many times identify with their profession, their identity strongly linked with what they do for a living. When someone asks them about themselves, they respond with their occupation. This link often translates into a strong attachment to their job. A man who is very attached to his job, if laid off, will go through a strong grief reaction. This reaction will be related to the degree of attachment he had in his identification with his job. It can also be related to his dependency on the job for maintaining his image of himself.

The variable of ambivalence tends to be more directly related to losses involving the death of someone who is close to us. In those situations our myriad of conflicting feelings complicate and prolong the grief. In situations like a job or other losses outside of an actual death, ambivalence plays less of a role. In the example of a job loss, it could be that a job we loved dearly would be more difficult to grieve than a job about which we had more ambivalence.

It is easy to see the relationship of naturalness and expectedness to the degree of grief in deaths by suicide and murder. There is usually no time to prepare for these losses, and they are off-the-scale when viewed in terms of naturalness. With these losses, it many times takes a person a year or so just to believe that the incident happened. It takes a certain amount of time just to incorporate the loss into their system, and the grief that follows is intensified and prolonged in relationship to the degree of expectedness and naturalness.

The variables spoken of in this chapter give us guidelines which can help us in evaluating our grief. They are not hard and fast rules. Grief is too murky and slippery to be pinned down with a few simple variables, but they do give us some idea about how to roughly gauge the intensity and duration of our grief.

3

Chaos And Ritual

When we experience a strong grief we will experience increased chaos in our lives. We are moved out of our routines and habits and thrust into a time and place that seems chaotic and unpredictable. What is this thing we are calling chaos? We can understand this a little better if we turn to nature as an example. All things in nature operate within a dynamic system. This dynamic system oscillates between two poles, stability and chaos. Stability is maintained for a period and then chaos is experienced, moving the system out of its patterns of stability and into something new, different, and life-changing. For instance, I have a favorite tree in my yard. This tree has a remarkably-shaped trunk, looking a little like a Coca-Cola bottle with a gaping wound wrapped around it. I have often wondered what brought the tree into this shape. Was it a massive vine, lightning, or disease? Whatever it was, it was chaos for the tree; it took the tree out of its stable growth pattern and changed its outward appearance and growth forever. You can think of the many trees in a forest and begin to get an idea of how the chaos they have experienced has shaped their growth and appearance. Each tree comes with its own ancestry from its seed and is then subject to the chaos of its location in the forest—from soil conditions to weather to amount of light to insects, fire, and the hand of man. Each tree moves in and out of the interplay of chaos and stability, producing its own unique essence.

People are also dynamic systems, and grief is a time when chaos is present in more than usual amounts. When we are out of our stable pattern, many things change. One of those changes is that we are extremely sensitized to even very tiny variables. Thus, people who are actively mourning speak of the smallest incidents sending them into a wave of grief. Examples such as hearing a particular song, or seeing a certain product in the grocery store, which normally would have no effect on a person in a stable pattern, suddenly can take on mammoth proportions. Hearing that song or seeing that product taps into the grief, and the grief is brought into consciousness in all of its fullness. This is the way of chaos.

It is natural for people, just as it is natural for all of nature, to be oscillating from stability to chaos. Grief is one of the times in a normal life cycle when we will experience more of this chaos than at others. Grief is not a pathological state; it is a normal life event that throws us into instability. This instability also has its own pattern, and if we look hard enough we may get a glimpse of it, a glimpse that shows the intricate pattern of the chaos itself. It is within this pattern that new and deeper parts of ourselves reside. Many times, however, the pattern of chaos is not noticed until years after the grief. The patterns of pain and chaos from our grief are a double-edged sword. They are painful and difficult, bringing chaos into our lives. But they also help us move into a more developed level of functioning.

Ritual and Sampling our Grief

What can be done to help us in dealing with this instability? In grief we need a way to access a small portion of our pain and chaos. What is needed is something to slowly and deliberately chip away at the grief, something to slowly dissipate it's power and resulting chaos. We can remember back to the story of the flute player in the first chapter. The flute player found a way to take a bit of the belly at a time. The way that we can do this for ourselves is through ritual. Ritual is a way for us to consciously take a small sample of our chaos, our grief, and to process that sample in our own time. By doing this, we get to know our grief and our chaos a little bit at a time. If we don't get to know it in some way, the chances are that the pressure of the chaos will build and the grief will spew forth at whatever time and in whatever manner it desires. Doing the sampling work will not stop the grief from coming forth unpredictably, but it will dissipate the pressure, much as a release valve in a steam engine does. The steam valve releases some of the pressure built up in the system—certainly not all of the pressure, but usually enough to let the system function. Grief rituals give us a way to release the chaos within our system a bit at a time, using the powerful resource of our own consciousness.

What is ritual? Firstly, it is important to note that ritual is a very difficult concept to define. We can begin by thinking of ritual as being a part of our everyday life. We practice it each day, but many of us are unaware of its presence. When broadly defined, ritual can be seen as a way of moving from one state of mind to another. Saying hello and good-bye are rudimentary forms of ritual in that they move us from one state to another, from being alone to being with someone and vice versa. By saying good-bye to someone as we get off the phone, we are marking a passage and experiencing a rudimentary ritual that mediates the transition from talking on the phone to hanging up. It is a culturally-sanctioned mechanism that smoothes the social movements of our lives.

There are many examples of this kind of ritual, from mealtimes to bedtimes. These everyday events that we practice are a kind of ritual that helps us in our daily living. Think of what you do to prepare for going to sleep, for example. What behaviors do you use to move from your waking state into a sleeping state? Most of us have personal rituals that we practice in this situation, such as putting on certain clothes, maybe listening to a radio program or reading, turning off the lights, reviewing the day's events, etc. Waking up in the morning is another example. That cup of coffee or a morning run are ways of moving from being in a state of sleep into a waking state. One's entire "morning routine" can be seen as a personal ritual that facilitates the transition from sleep to wakefulness.

Grief rituals are both similar and different in some respects to these everyday rituals. One of the differences is that the rituals we have mentioned thus far are mostly related to habits that we have developed to help us in transitions. These habits, although helpful, are a part of our daily routine. In grief rituals, unlike our previously mentioned habits, we are practicing behaviors that <u>consciously</u> and <u>intentionally</u> move us out of our ordinary awareness and into the experience of the pain of grief. We use these rituals as a mechanism to consciously move into our chaos and our pain. Much as the flute player in the first chapter used his knife to cut a bit of the snake, people find mechanisms to cut away a bit of the belly a small chunk at a time.

Grief rituals are not esoteric practices. They are something that you are probably already doing for yourself in your daily living. They can be as simple as leafing through a photo album or as complex as writing a symphony. The important thing is that the ritual activity is intended to connect you with your pain and grief and allows you to move out of ordinary awareness and into the experience of grief, in a safe way, for a period of time.

Ritual and its Structure

All ritual has an underlying structure. This structure describes the active components in the ritual, not the details of a personal ritual, but the infrastructure that lies beneath the surface. By knowing the components of the infrastructure you will be able to use this knowledge as a means to both understand the ritual you may already be doing for yourself, as well as be able to create new rituals that will fit your needs. The importance of understanding ritual in grieving is that it gives us a workable outline of how to heal from a painful loss. This knowledge is similar to what a good grief therapist would be conscious of during therapy.

In our culture, where there are almost no sanctioned rituals for healing grief, we are forced into a position of having to create our own rituals, many times without the help of others. The following will describe what I mean by ritual and will give examples of how this ritual process is used in healing grief.

Containment

To see what the elements of ritual are let's look at a simplified example. Think of the last time you went to an amusement park. Remember all the rides you went on or just watched. Almost all the rides at the park are "containers" for chaos. Consider a roller coaster: the speed and curves and loops of a roller coaster are certainly chaotic. Think of the situation you would be in if you had no bar locking you into your seat, no sides to the car, or worse yet, no tracks for the car to ride. The train itself is a container in which you ride through the chaos. Without that container you would be in trouble. The container of the roller coaster gives you a vessel within which you can experience safely the chaos of the ride. Many of the other rides in the amusement park are like this. A giant water slide, some 70 feet tall with a drop that seems to be straight down, comes to mind. As you pick up speed and rush down the slope, the water and the sides of the slide "contain" the experience for you. What otherwise might be a fatal drop becomes a contained experience of chaos.

The first element of ritual then is the idea of a container. Just as in an amusement park ride, ritual gives us a container in which to experience safely the chaos of grief. When grieving, we look for containers much like those in the amusement park—something with sides on it and a handle to grab if we need. Containment means creating a space where ritual will allow the chaos to be workable. People speak of this space as being "contained space." Psychotherapy offers a good example of contained space.[2] In therapy, the hour of time together is not supposed to be ordinary time, but an hour when the client feels that he is in contained space. Think of the elements of therapy. The therapist agrees not to make public anything that goes on in the treatment room. The client can feel that he is safe to talk about things without having to worry about content or breach of confidentiality. The client should feel that the therapist has his best interests at heart, that he is not in danger, and is free to be his genuine self, not just his mask self. Contained space in healing grief is simply a safe place to process the grief within. It is the first step in healing, for without it healing will not take place.

The idea of contained space also gives us a beginning understanding of the differences between men and women in grief. People naturally look for a safe place in which to experience the chaos of grief, but men and women tend to find safety in very different places. A woman often finds safety in her relationships with others and in relating the pain of her grief to those to whom she is close. A man, on the other hand, does not generally see this kind of space as being particularly safe. He will tend (for many reasons) to seek a more private and action-oriented container. It is not, as many people think, that the man doesn't grieve. He merely seeks a different type of contained space.

Some people have described contained space (and ritual) as being like an oven. This is not a normal, everyday environment, but one which requires a steward. In psychotherapy the therapist has to decide how long and at what temperature the client should remain in the "oven" of contained space. It is the responsibility of the therapist to maintain a proper environment for the client. In essence, he acts as a "ritual elder" in containing the space. The ritual elder, or person who stewards the contained space, is usually someone who has experienced the chaos himself on many occasions and knows the ins and outs of it. He is there to set up and maintain the container for the person going through the ritual. Aside from psychotherapists and ministers or spiritual teachers, ritual elders are scarce in our culture. As we have become increasingly technological we have moved farther and farther away from contact with ritual. It is almost as if we assume that we can think our way out of everything, that logic and technology can supply an answer to every problem. We might even tend to see ritual as superstitious or primitive. This scarcity of ritual and ritual elders leaves us in a serious state of affairs when it comes to grief. Most of us are left to our own devices when it comes to healing our grief, without the compassionate guidance of an elder and without the socially-sanctioned mechanisms of ritual.

Submission

Thus, the first two elements of ritual are containment—an enclosure within which the ritual can be effective—and a ritual elder or guide to direct and watch over the process. Once these two elements are in place, other factors come into play, the first of which is submission. In order for the ritual to be effective one must submit to the process of chaos. Without submission the ritual can go only a small distance in healing. In the example of the roller coaster ride, submission would be getting into the seat, locking yourself in, and taking the ride. A lack of submission would be not getting into the seat. You might have the roller coaster at your disposal but if you don't lock into the seat you will never enter the chaos. In grieving, a lack of submission is usually a refusal to allow the chaos of grief into your consciousness. It is saying "no" to the grief. The primary reason for this is that the container does not feel safe enough.

An example of submission in ritual space might be an Alcoholics Anonymous meeting. The meeting itself is the contained space, and the element of submission is evidenced by the participant's opening statement, "My name is Bob, and I'm an alcoholic." The statement "I'm an alcoholic" begins the submission to chaos. The participant often goes on to say something such as "I am powerless in the face of alcohol." This is submission: I am powerless against these forces.

Therapists sometimes talk of the resistance of a client to therapy. This is a lack of submission. As a therapist, I have grown to know that many times it is more useful to change the container of therapy and somehow make it safer, rather than force the client to submit to the therapeutic container that I think is best.

Deconstruction

What happens during ritual once you have a contained space, a ritual elder, and a participant who has submitted to the process? The next element of ritual is called deconstruction. For our purposes, deconstruction is when a person "takes apart" the old self that they inhabited before the loss. At the risk of making grief too concrete, we can think of this taking apart roughly in the same vein as fixing something that is malfunctioning. You might think of a time when your car didn't start. What you probably did was check the battery connections, then the battery itself, and maybe looked into the distributor, or pulled the spark plugs. In the process of taking things apart, or deconstructing, you found that one of the spark plugs was fouled. You then realized that this was the probable cause for the car's not starting. This process of taking things apart is in some ways similar to the process of deconstruction within ritual space.

In grief the deconstruction that takes place is the taking apart of the old self and the old desires. It is the observance of the death of one's old self. This is done within a contained space and, ideally, under the watchful eye of a ritual elder. I say ideally because, as we have noted, our culture has very few ritual elders. As we will see, most of the rituals that men in our culture have created to contain their grief are solo efforts. They do not have the luxury of a mentor stewarding the process.

Reconstruction

After the deconstruction process the last phase of ritual takes place. This phase is reconstruction. After we have taken apart the old and identified what is in need of change, we are able to build a new part to replace it. In the example of the car, it would be simply putting in a new spark plug. In grief it is not so simple. There are many aspects of ourselves that are in need of deconstruction and reconstruction and the process is not linear. By this, I mean that in the first month of grief we might go through the process of deconstructing and reconstructing some aspect of our grief, but it might be a year or two before some other aspect is integrated. In reconstructing we go through the many parts of ourselves that are affected by the grief. These can include our roles at work or home, our identifications with people or things, our habits, attitudes, or feelings.

An example of this might be a habit you had of calling your wife each day at two o'clock. Two months after she died, you dial the number at two o'clock and realize as the phone rings that no one is going to answer. Your secretary announces over the intercom that your two o'clock appointment has arrived, but you say that you are running late. You shut the door and are engulfed in feelings of sadness. You may cry some, then tell yourself "okay, pull yourself together," and you get ready for your appointment. This process is ritual in microcosm: by shutting your door you have created the closest thing to a contained space you could; by allowing the feelings of sadness to be conscious you are entering the chaos; by crying you are deconstructing. The tears are the expression of the pain of the grief. You are releasing the pain associated with this loss, and therefore deconstructing. Each time you do this you are closer to a point of being able to reconstruct new habits that are not based on the old self. By "pulling yourself together" you are leaving the contained space and re-entering the ordinary world.

Rituals Around the World

We can learn more about ritual by taking a look at a few examples from around the world. In tribal cultures there are time-honored rituals with which to enter contained space and deal with one's chaos. Rituals such as initiation ceremonies where the boy becomes a man or the girl a woman show the elements of ritual we have just discussed. The male ritual of initiation, for example, is crafted to be a contained space for the chaos of the death of the boy and the birth of the man. The boy takes part in a community-accepted ritual that will see him as a man after his ordeal. By dying to his boyhood, the boy enters chaos and deconstructs that part of himself, then gives birth to and reconstructs the man within himself by entering manhood. He begins the process of identifying with the man within. The power of this kind of sanctioned ritual is not to be underestimated. Not only does the boy have the experience of the ritual, but he is surrounded by a community that has a deep respect for this process and most likely sees the ritual as analogous to reality, if not reality itself. The community sees him now as a man, and this brings power to the ritual and its effects. The grief process is similar to this ritual: we die to the old self and give birth to a new one.

Another example comes from India. When a Hindu monk takes his vows, a part of the ceremony is a funeral for his former self. The old self dies. The monk is given a new name in the Swami order, and the date of his initiation is now considered his birthday. He is literally reborn on the day of his initiation, and his former self is considered dead.

Rituals in our own Culture

All of these examples are from other cultures. What happens in our own culture to men when they are grieving? The answer is a bit surprising. Men and women in our culture also use ritual in healing their grief. Without the structure of a culturally-sanctioned ritual for healing grief, we are put in a position of needing to create our own rituals. The men and women of our culture have done this, and the ways they have accomplished this are as varied as the people themselves. Each person seems to find their own way to use ritual. It depends on the strengths and weaknesses of the individual. People will tend to practice rituals that align with their strength in order to make contact with their chaos in a safe way.

Delano Foster

An example of the utilization of a grief ritual is the experience of Delano Foster, a grief therapist in Washington, D. C., who works with families whose relatives have been murdered.[3] A year and a half ago, Foster's own brother was murdered. Delano grieved in many ways, but of particular interest to us is that he built a pond in honor of his brother. He dedicated the pond to his brother and erected a plaque in his honor. The pond became a place that reminded him of his brother and his own pain related to his brother's death. Whenever Delano is sitting at the pond he is closer to the experience of grief from his brother's death and the resulting chaos, and the pond becomes a ritual space for him to process his grief. Both the building of the pond and the time he spends there can be rituals that help him move out of his ordinary awareness and into his pain.

Brad Hamann

Another man, Brad Hamann, described his grief ritual in an article in *Runners World.*[4] He and his father were running the New York Marathon together. As Brad crossed the finish line, he learned that his father had died of a heart attack at a certain point in the race. The son took from his father's wrist the runner's watch that he had been wearing. The watch became a symbol of both his grief and his father's life and death. He kept it in his desk drawer and would choose certain times to take it out and look at it, still running on the stop watch cycle. The watch and the times he would take it out and observe it became his contained space. He chose the times to do this, and each time he did he created a contained space for himself to deconstruct and then reconstruct. As he pulled the watch from the drawer, he left his ordinary awareness and entered into the chaos of grief. His feelings for his father would arise and be honored and acknowledged by him. He didn't go to therapy or join a grief group, but he found a way to create a contained space for himself and to gradually heal from this loss. The next year he ran the marathon again, wearing both his own and his father's watch. After starting the race he approached a bridge, and describing himself as spontaneously knowing what to do, he threw his father's old watch into the river. He knew that he had reconstructed enough to abandon this contained space and this old symbol.

Paul

Let's take a different example. A man I know used his exercise program, his running, as a container for his grief. His name was Paul and his father's death had left him with a good deal of grief. Paul found he could contain and heal his grief through running. As he went out each day, and sometimes twice a day, he would use that contained space to process the thoughts and feelings that arose. He lived next to a park and he would run through the park. As he did this, feelings of grief would arise. He talked about crying buckets as he ran, of needing windshield wipers to see where he was going. He found himself running more and more each day. Paul was using his running as a contained space for his grief. It is not well known, but many men use running in the same way Paul did. Getting out of the house and into a quiet place is creating the container. Submitting to the process while in that space allows the emergence of feelings and thoughts related to the grief. Paul used this ritual repeatedly as he slowly healed his grief.

We can see how these men used ritual in healing their grief. They created spaces in which they felt comfortable and safe in tapping into the chaos of their grief. Paul did this with his running, Delano by building a pond, and Brad used his father's watch. There was no ritual elder to steward the process; they did this for themselves. I do know that in Paul's case, he spoke with other men about his process of running and grieving which further released the pressure of the grief he was experiencing. These men allowed their contained space to be a place where they could submit to their chaos, and deconstruct and reconstruct. It is important to note that they found their chosen ritual path on their own, without the help of others. There is a wide variety of paths such as these that men in our culture take in healing their grief.

I do not want to imply in this book that men shouldn't seek out help in dealing with their grief. The healing of a man's grief is aided by contact with other men (or women), and from contact with a good grief therapist. Grief is like manure: if you spread it out, it fertilizes; if you leave it in a big pile, it smells like hell. When we are in a strong grief process we can use all of the support we can get. If you are a man and decide to go into therapy, I strongly suggest that you seek out a male therapist who has plenty of experience in dealing with grief and who will let you use him as a consultant. I have found that men prefer a consulting arrangement where they have more say in the times they choose to consult.

Summary

The framework of ritual—contained space, submission, deconstruction, and reconstruction—can give men and women an outline to evaluate their own ways of healing. Grief is a process that demands ritual. When we experience a loss, we are stunned and enter into chaos. If the loss is large enough and crosses our threshold of tolerance, then we also submit. As we have seen, most people are naturally drawn to seek out a safe, contained space for grieving that fits with their own strengths and weaknesses. By consciously practicing our own personal rituals, we can slowly diminish the pressure of our grief and open ourselves to the chaos within. We can safely receive both the trauma and the gift that grief brings us.

4

Standing in
Your Tension

You are walking by the ocean. As you walk you notice
the cliff behind you, the trees and rocks jutting out
from the side of the cliff. The trees are twisted and gnarled
as if they were attempting to escape the ground in which they grow.
That, in fact, is what they are doing, for they have seen Sisiutl.
Sisiutl is the monster from the sea, a hideous-looking creature with
two heads. When anyone sees Sisiutl there is only one response:
total fear. The urge to run is uncontrollable, it is blinding, the only
thing one can think of is to run as fast and far as possible, and not to
look back. This is the way it is when one sees Sisiutl.

Suddenly, out in the ocean, you see Sisiutl. Your entire body reacts
automatically and wants to run, but you stand firm. You know if
you run you will never stop running, you will be like the twisted
trees on the cliff attempting to leave the ground in which you stand,
so you stand firm. Sisiutl comes in closer, you can see his two
heads waving above the surface of the ocean. Now he is close
enough for you to smell his foul stench and you utter prayers of

protection as he moves in. With one more wave he will be upon you. He lets out a screeching sound, both heads approaching you from either side. It's too late to run; fear washes over you. Just as the heads are inches away from your own head, they stop. Both of Sisiutl's heads stare into the other's eyes. He stops and stares.

Sisiutl searches far and wide for anyone who will stand firm so he can glimpse his other side. When his other side is seen, truth is given to the one who stands firm in that tension. Whenever you stand firm like this, you will be visited by the vision people, and they will show you truth.[5]

This story gives us a glimpse of the essence of healing from grief. Grief can be like seeing Sisiutl, wanting to run as fast and as far as possible. In order to heal we must find a way to stand in our own tension. A summary of this process might be as follows. A man finds his strength, and then uses that strength (usually an action) to connect with his grief and pain. He then chooses to stand in that pain and grief, standing his ground for periods at a time. The following section will describe many ideas about standing in our tension and how to do that. It will examine the things that hinder us from making a good connection with our grief and some of the prerequisites of making that connection with Sisiutl.

Becoming Aware of Grief

The first thing that can make it difficult for men to stand their ground is the process of becoming acutely aware of the grief. Many times, if the grief is not overwhelming us and demanding our attention, it is lurking within us like a shadow, unnamed but affecting our moods and behavior all the same. Often, we can sense that something is different, but we are not sure exactly what it is. Sometimes it takes feedback from others that there is something different about us in order for us to be aware of this difference. This was the case with Ron.

Ron's father had died several months before. He was aware of some of his sadness, but didn't think much about it. His wife kept telling him he was in a foul mood, but he told her she was the one who was cranky. One day while working at his computer, he opened a drawer in the computer hutch and noticed a pair of ticket stubs from the all-star game he and his father had attended years ago. He sat quietly for a while and memories of his father arose. He thought of his father and the things they had done together, of the many ways in which he missed his father. He noticed a heavy feeling in his chest and focused his attention on that sensation. As he did, tears formed in his eyes, and something started to flow from his chest up through his head. He allowed himself to "stand" in that moment and experience what was there.

Ron had found his grief. The tickets were a stimulus to finding his tension, and once found, he had chosen to stand in it. In order to do this he had to do several things. The first was to slow down. Men tend to be outer directed and goal oriented, on the go much of the time. Grief needs a slow pace, a pause that refreshes. We need to find a way to slow down in order to see that Sisiutl is lurking within us. Sitting quietly and just observing our inner process is a big help in starting to work with our grief.

Being in the body is the second requirement. Ron did this by observing the sensation in his chest. The tickets brought the memories up; Ron was aware of his body, and the grief flowed. Often a man connects with his grief by his awareness of his body.

One man I worked with described his personal sensation as being like a "black hole" in his stomach, another said it was like a wave that rolled up from his gut. These sensations are like markers that aid a man in connecting to his grief.

This need for calmness and being aware of one's body can be seen in the difficulty some people experience with not being able to get to sleep. The process of falling asleep demands that we get in touch with our bodies enough to make ourselves relatively comfortable. It also asks us to slow down our inner and outer pace. This slowing down makes us more sensitized to whatever might have been bubbling beneath our conscious surface. In the case of grief, if we have been avoiding our grief during the day and not giving it our attention, when we go to bed it will find just the right conditions to surface. Many people I have worked with have experienced this phenomenon of having the grief arise just as they are going to sleep. This produces considerable frustration and sleepless nights and can be diminished if we learn to give this same kind of quiet space to our grief during the day.

Not Grieving Brings Dark Moods

When we are not in touch with our grief, we will tend to be moody and cranky, what some Jungians call a dark mood. Men get these dark moods when they have an overload of feelings but have not found a way to stand in their tension. What usually happens is that the man gets cranky, bitter, resentful, and proceeds to blame the nearest woman for this mood he is in. John Sanford in his book *The Invisible Partners* describes this as a dark mood that grips the man.[6]

For the sake of balance, I want to point out that in the case of a woman not dealing with her grief a similar thing can happen. She often takes on a self-righteous, pompous, know-it-all kind of stance.

She has all the answers to all the questions, if only people would listen to her. Shoulds and shouldn'ts are freely distributed. She is frustrated that the world is not listening to her solutions.

When we find our grief, we are at least partially released from the grip of this dark mood. As I have said before, grief is like manure: if you spread it out, it fertilizes; if you leave it in a big pile, it smells like hell. In order to spread out our grief and use it as fertilizer, we need to slow down and be aware of our body. When we do this, we can begin to name that which is within. When Ron experienced the tears for his father, he then had an experience that connected him to his grief. He could name it. As soon as you name something, you begin to have power over it. Think of how difficult different aspects of life would be if you didn't have names for things. Imagine going into the grocery store and not knowing the name of anything you needed to buy. Or spending the rest of your life in a foreign country and never learning the language. This is in some ways similar to people who have not named their grief.

The story of James will serve as an example. After his father's death, James was aware of something different inside him, but he couldn't seem to catch it's essence. One day James decided he would just sit with this unnamed thing and get to know it. He sat in his den quietly and used his conscious awareness to track this part of himself. After about 15 minutes of sitting, things started to take shape. James realized that the unnamed guest was a nagging feeling of sadness related to his father's death. When he examined it closely, he realized that he could almost hear it talk. It was saying to him that he missed his father, wanted his father to return, and was afraid that he was not "good enough" to take over the role of elder in his extended family. These realizations were not a surprise to James, but they were now brought into focus and named, and thus became something he could work *with* rather than something that worked *on* him.

Grief as a Guest

James called these feelings "guests," and in many ways grief is like a guest. You are not the grief. The grief is residing in you for a period of time. The mistake many people make with grief is to become identified with the feelings of grief to the point of thinking that they *are* the grief. During a strong grief reaction, which can last for many years, men and women begin to think that the feelings are a permanent fixture inside them, that they are never going to go away. Soon these people believe that since the feelings are not going away, they must be them. This starts a process within the person of resignation, of giving up. We can remember the flute player from a previous chapter, who was trapped in the belly of a giant boa constrictor and found himself able to take a small chunk out of the snake's belly, a bit at a time. When we are in the situation where we start to give up, it is as if the snake (the grief) were saying "Just lie down and be digested—there is no way out of here." We start to think that we are the snake. This is analogous to thinking we are what we just ate. In the morning we eat breakfast, let's say a bowl of cereal. Do you think at mid-day that you are that bowl of cereal? The food is a part of you now, it is inside of you, but is it really you? I think not, and grief is similar. In the same way, grief is a temporary resident that needs to be digested and excreted. It is not you, it is a temporary part of you.

The Persona and Grief

One of the reasons that men in our culture are so susceptible to this identification with feelings is that men generally have a very strong persona. The persona is the part of us that acts as our mask. It is the presenting front that we want people to see, that for many males in our culture shows us as competent individuals who are independent and strong. This is not the real self, but only a part of ourselves. It is the part that says "image is everything," as the commercial says. It is also the part of us that "breaks down" when grief erupts. No longer can we maintain a front of being strong and independent, for our culture dictates that a man's strength is related to how stoic he can be. This is why we call it "breaking down." We are not really breaking down; we are merely accessing a different part of our psyche. The more men are identified with their persona, the more difficult it will be to access easily various parts of our grief. This is because the persona doesn't want to have anything to do with grief. Grief is seen many times as a sign of weakness and something to be avoided. We need to come to an agreement with our persona about when and how we will be able to access our grief.

The Pain of Pain

As we do access our feeling states, we need to keep in mind that while we want to experience the pain of our grief, just as importantly, we want to avoid the pain of pain. This is what happens when we start feeling bad about feeling bad. Instead of a direct experience of our pain, we go to a secondary level and start to experience the pain indirectly. This problem is similar to the snake eating its tail. It is as if we are chewing on ourselves. If you experience the pain of grief, you will slowly heal, but if you get into the pain of pain, it can continue *ad infinitum*. The pain can become a self-perpetuating machine that will slowly grind you up. It is bad enough to have to go through the pain of grief without going through the pain of pain.

The example of Jim illustrates this idea. Jim had experienced the death of his wife several months ago. He was doing his best to take care of his children and make enough money to keep his family going. Jim was experiencing overwhelming periods of grief where he felt like he was just trying to keep himself above water. He then began berating himself for having these periods, calling himself names and evaluating himself as a less than adequate man. This is the pain of pain, when we feel bad about feeling bad. Keep a watchful eye out for this monster.

Grief is Healed

To summarize then, grief is healed when we are able to courageously stand in it and not run. When we are able to name it and start to know its comings and goings. When we are able to slow down our pace and find a place to experience our pain within. When we are able to be in our body. When we are able to accept it as a temporary visitor and not think that we are that grief. When we are able to make an agreement with the part of ourselves that is the mask self, in order to access our pain. And when we can discriminate between the pain of grief and the pain of pain.

5

The Experience
of Emotions in Grief

This chapter will focus on the primary feelings of grief: anger, sadness, guilt, and helplessness. These are not the totality of the feeling states of grief, but they do represent the major building blocks. As we explore these different feelings, we will look at how each one is easy or not so easy for men.

Anger

Anger is often a part of grief. The following describes the expression of anger among the men of the Cubeo Indians when an old man of their tribe dies:

The old woman, truly grief stricken, had embraced her dead husband's body in the hammock and rocked over it, moaning and wailing. She withdrew however, when the younger brother of (the old man) arrived. He felt for the heartbeat and then covered the old man's face with some rags that had been the sick man's blanket.

The women had all gathered to one side of the hammock and wept continuously, chorusing the loud and emphatic wailing of the widow. The brother fetched his shotgun, moving slowly and grimly. He loaded it with a wad, and turned to face the corpse. Each man now went with the same slow deliberateness to fetch his gun. The armed men formed a tight circle around the hammock, the widow in their midst pressed against it. Brandishing the weapon, the brother began the funeral declamation, a statement of grief and then anger and the threat of retaliation against the enemy. Each male mourner delivered his own address, always declaring his kinship relationship to the old man. The women accompanied the hoarse shouts of masculine anger with their own counterpoint of grief. After the last man had spoken they all fired their guns into the air together. The widow then withdrew to her hammock and lay silently while the men gathered about the hammock, caressed the corpse, and wept, accompanied in their grief by the women.[7]

The Cubeo men were able to find a way to express their anger at something that they could not see or control. This is many times the way it is with grief. The anger we feel is usually directed at something that is not visible (God?) or something beyond our control. This anger is a very important part of a man's grief.

Anger as a Path to Grief

The expression of anger seems more natural for men than expressing other feelings. When expressing anger, we need to take a stand, to define our ground. This is quite different from the mechanics of sadness, which require a more open and vulnerable stance. It is important to note that men in our culture will sometimes find their other feelings of grief through their anger. Many times in working with men I have found that while a man is expressing anger (and I mean really expressing it.....loudly, with movement of the body, etc.), he suddenly will be moved to tears. It is almost as if touching on that profound and deep feeling of anger has brought him in touch with his other feelings. This process is reversed with women. Many times a woman would be in tears, crying and crying. I might ask what her tears are about, and she often would state plainly and many times loudly "I'm angry."

A person's anger during grief can range from being angry with the person who died to being angry with God, and all points in between. My mentor, Father William Wendt, once told me a story about anger and grief. It seems that Bill had been visiting a widow and working with her on her grief. He noticed that many times when he arrived she was driving her car up and down the driveway. One day he asked her what she was doing. She proceeded to tell him that she had a ritual she used in dealing with her grief. She would come home, go to the living room, and get her recently deceased husband's ashes out of the urn on the mantle. She would take a very small amount and place them on the driveway. She then told Bill that, "It helps me to run over the son of a bitch every day." Bill concluded the story by saying, "Now that is good grief."

Bill thought it was "good" grief because it was this woman's way of connecting to and expressing the anger component of her grief.

Releasing Anger Through Ritual

Another example comes from an African tribe where the story is told that after a man's son died, he took his bow and arrows deep into the jungle and proceeded to shoot his entire stock of arrows into the air in all directions. This was his ritual for expressing his anger at that moment. Instead of acting it out in an unproductive way, such as picking a fight or becoming negative and sarcastic, he found a meaningful way to release his anger.

I once worked with a man who, after the death of his infant son, bought a cheap set of china, went to the city dump, and proceeded to bust each and every piece of it. This was his way of expressing the same thing that the African man did with his bow and arrows. He found a way to safely express the rage he felt, and he did so privately without involving other people.

Another example was related to me by a friend who was giving a weekend workshop for about twenty-five people. Two or three hours prior to the end of the weekend, my friend received a phone call informing him that one participant's brother had died suddenly and unexpectedly. My friend went to this man, a middle-aged man from Brazil, and told him about his brother's death. The man stopped for a moment, and after some initial emotion and disbelief, asked if six of the male participants could come outside with him. The women, he said, were to stay in the building. The seven men went outside together. The man instructed each of the six to hold him by the arms and legs and to not let go. He then placed a rolled up piece of cloth in his mouth and bit down on this as he proceeded to struggle against the resistance the six men provided. As he struggled, he screamed and moaned. This went on for some time until the man was exhausted. With the help of the other participants, this man was able to create a spontaneous ritual to give him some vent for his overwhelming feelings. He was able to find a ritual that would allow him to express on the outside what his feeling state was on the inside.

Men and the Protective Mode of Grief

Men around the world have developed various means to deal with their anger relating to their grief. Rosenblatt's study of cross-cultural grief points out that it is consistent across different cultures that men will express more anger than women during grief, particularly if it is focused outside the self.[8] We see this in the African archer and the man with his set of china. I had the good fortune to meet Malidoma Some, the author of *Ritual: Power, Healing, and Community*, which describes the grief rituals of his native people, the Dagura of Africa.[9] Malidoma explained to me that the men of his tribe grieve in what he called the "protective" mode, patterned after the masculine modeling of the behavior of the father. The women, he said, grieved in the "nurturing" mode, patterned after the behavior of the mother. He went on to say that the protective mode of grief was many times associated with anger, whereas the nurturing mode was connected more to nurturing and caring. It seems to me that these two modes Malidoma describes are easily seen in the way men and women heal from their grief in our own culture. The men sometimes find their path to their grief through anger, the women through sadness. This is a gross generalization on my part, but on the whole I feel there is truth in it.

The act of a man's consciously dealing with his anger during grief is many times instrumental in his path toward healing. It can also have many other benefits. We have already seen the benefit of putting a man in touch with other deep feeling states, but there is more. One obvious plus is that what you are on the outside is in harmony with what you feel on the inside. This is not to be minimized. The denial of chronic feeling states is a dangerous thing and leaves people in perpetual states of needing to live a lie. This living a lie has big effects on our psyche. It cuts us off from the world around us and limits our capacity to relate to others. If we are busy in maintaining a false image, we will not be able to be in the present tense, for we will always be jumping ahead and preparing for the next contingency. "To thine own self be true" is an important maxim.

Hostility *versus* Anger

In an article published in the *New York Times* December 13, 1990, the authors described an eighteen year study of hostility and it's affects on health. The study found that those having a high hostility rate were five times more likely to have an early death than those with a low hostility rating. It has been my experience that those people with a high hostility rate are many times those people who are not dealing with their anger, and due to this, are misdirecting this anger out to various targets that are only tangentially associated with the original feeling. By dealing with one's anger we can avoid this dilemma of long-term hostility. But hostility is not the only means of misdirecting anger. Anger not channeled consciously can come out in all sorts of ways. The possibilities might include: being silent, being negative and sarcastic, exaggerated upset over a trivial irritation, and getting other people upset (to relieve your own anger). It seems more productive to use bow and arrows or china.

Another plus of consciously dealing with our anger is that we are then afforded the opportunity to redirect that energy into other aspects of our life. Anger is a powerful source of energy that we lose if our rage becomes unconscious. There are countless examples of men being able to redirect their rage into productive outlets. Martin Luther King is an obvious example. He was able to harness his anger and that of others into a national movement that changed the social fabric of our country. This same thing can be done by any of us, maybe not on a national level but certainly on a personal level. Men I have known have spoken of this sort of thing. One man was furious, but aware of it, and proceeded to chop his entire supply of wood for the winter. That is putting the anger to work. It is important to note that many times the conscious expression of feelings for men involves some sort of activity, and many times using the body (chopping wood) is integrated into the expression. This is in contrast to a woman's tendency to relate her feelings verbally to those to whom she feels close.

Expectation and Hurt

A way to bring anger into conscious awareness is to attempt to break it down into its various components. Anger is most times related to *desire*. Flowing from the desire is our attachment to preconceived *expectations* about the way things should or shouldn't be. For most of us, if our expectations are not met, we will feel *hurt*. As an example, imagine you have made an agreement with your wife about spending money. The budget is tight and you have agreed to limit your personal spending to a certain amount. You find out that your wife has spent far beyond the limit. You are angry. You *expected* that your wife would honor your agreement and she didn't. You feel *hurt* that she could treat you in this way when you have both agreed to a mutual limit. This element of being hurt is the connection between sadness and anger. In fact, if you look at almost any angry reaction you might have, there is usually a kernel of sadness and hurt. So the components of anger generally break down to expectation and hurt. Think about the last time you were really angry. Why were you angry? Now think of the expectation you had that was not met. Think of the way you felt in response to not having your expectation met—probably angry and hurt. If we can understand these elements, we will be in better shape to address and channel our anger. We don't want to think or theorize it away, just begin to understand it. Then we are in a position to use our anger productively. This idea of expectation and hurt also helps in communicating the anger to another person, in a way that is expressive of your inner feeling and can be heard by others. Having a conflict and standing your ground over whether your expectation was reasonable is almost always a productive conflict, whereas the expression of hostility tends to lead to misunderstanding and more hurt and distance.

Sadness

Sadness has a bad name in our culture. It has taken on a connotation of something to be avoided, something that is unacceptable to express. This is significantly different from the meaning of one of the roots of the word "sad," that being the same as the word "satisfied" or "sate." In Old English it meant literally "fullness of heart." And as we see by the Inuit tale, "First Man," a full heart soon overflows:

One day first man went out seal hunting along a seashore. He saw many seals. He chose a seal, and carefully crept up behind it, but with a splash it tumbled into the water. He looked around and found another seal, and crept up towards it even more carefully, but just as he was about to reach it, it too splashed into the water.

This went on and on. At last there was only one seal left on the rocks. Man thought that this time he would be so quiet that the seal would notice nothing, but as soon as he began to move toward it, it slid off the rocks and swam away.

Then man stood up and in his chest he felt a strange feeling. The strange feeling seemed to fill all the space in his chest. Suddenly, water began to run from his eyes. The drops of water ran from his eyes and down his face. When he felt them he put up his hand and felt some of the drops. He looked at them. They really were water. Then, without knowing what he was going to do, or without wanting to do it, he felt loud cries breaking from him. As he headed for home, the loud cries continued, and the water went on running down his face.

When man's son saw him coming he called to his wife and to his mother. "Look" he said, "here comes man making such a strange noise." When man came closer they were all surprised to see the water running down his face. But after he told them the story of the seals, they were all stricken with the same strange sickness, and they began to wail along with him. And this is the way people first learned how to cry.[10]

Sadness and Grief

Sadness is an integral part of grief, and tears are an integral part of sadness. I know of no more efficient method to deal with our sadness consciously than to cry through it. Tears in grief are healing, although many times people have a sense that the tears will never end. This fear stops some people from accessing their sadness. We shudder when we get that full feeling in our chest, and we turn away from the expression of that sensation. This turning away starts to set up a habit of stuffing our grief. The very tool we have to mend our pain is what we turn away from. Why do we turn away from tears?

Provider/Protector Role and Sadness

Men have been put at a disadvantage when it comes to using this powerful resource of crying. We are all aware of how men are taught not to cry and how our society discourages men from the public expression of tears. But there are other reasons that men have a hard time in shedding tears. One is that men are in a double bind.[11] At home they are seen as the provider and protector. When a time of grief comes, men are expected to be, and usually want to be, involved in these roles. However, the roles of protector and provider don't mix well with the expression of tears. The expression of tears requires a safe place, a place where we feel there is containment. By containment I mean that we know that someone or something will be there to pull us out of the fire if we get too burnt or will let us stay in the fire if we haven't cooked enough. We are expected to be the "strong ones," and the strong ones aren't expected to be vulnerable and in a state of need themselves. A man's role in the family is often to "contain" the space, or make it safe for the members of his own family. So men get caught between the need to cry and the roles of provider/protector, and they don't expect anyone else to provide a safe space for them. When you couple this with the conditioning men have received, the probability of a man crying openly at home is significantly diminished. This is one of the reasons men are left without the resource of open mourning and thus tend to use a more private and active approach to their grief.

When men do cry at home, they are sometimes putting themselves in jeopardy. This problem often comes up when I work with families who have experienced a major loss. Sometimes the family members complain that the man is not openly mourning. The man has been seeing to it that the other family members could grieve (Malidoma's protective mode of grief?), but is not openly grieving himself. With a great deal of pressure from the family, the father finally openly mourns. Yet the power of the father's tears and mourning usually shocks the family. The children are often upset to see their father cry. They describe the episodes in disbelief and shock. They are openly frank about their fears of seeing their father cry and describe how scary it is to see the person they view as the foundation of their life in a state of grief. The men in this situation are leaving the protector/provider role, and the result is that the family experiences anxiety at the loss of that function. They no longer have the protector. This masculine function often goes unnoticed until it disappears. The wife, too, is often a bit upset. Usually she is ambivalent; on one hand she is relieved to see her husband cry, but on the other hand she is uncomfortable with it, feeling somehow insecure and even afraid.   The men can feel their family's ambivalence towards their behavior and will seek out a safe place to emote. In addition, the men often quickly realize the discomfort of others with their tears, and this solidifies their solitary grief. This does not seem so unusual to me considering the circumstances, but the media and many mental health professionals are continually condemning men for their private grief. Perhaps a man's stewarding and protecting his family can be seen as one way for him to honor his own grief.

A part of the family's shock at seeing the father cry may be related to the newness of the experience. Perhaps if the men had gradually been more emotional prior to the crisis of grief, the spouse and children would not have been so upset. Even with this being so, the men were not in the same state of need prior to the crisis. In a healthy family unit there needs to be a sharing of the protector/provider role as it relates to containing a space for emotional expression. If you are a man and you are able to cry, consider yourself blessed. If you can cry, and have someone near you who can comfortably honor and contain that, consider yourself twice blessed.

Sadness and the Hierarchy

Another element involved in a man's lack of tears is his need for respect. For a man to be vulnerable in front of another, he needs to feel that he has the respect of that individual. This need is related to a man's hierarchical nature and his fear that if he shows vulnerability he will tumble to the bottom of the hierarchy. This differs from the woman's need. The woman needs a sense that the other person wants to relate to her. You can see this difference in many marriages. So many times the woman is yearning for the man to relate to her, and the man is reacting to situations where he feels he is not getting enough respect.

Connecting Sadness and the Body

Grief is no respector of a man's need for respect, however. No longer do we have a choice about stuffing this or that feeling, or putting something off. Grief demands emoting, and it demands it not on our time schedule, but on its own. As this happens, we begin to get to know that "strange feeling" in the chest more intimately just as the seal hunter did. As with anger, a man will many times connect with his sadness through his body. A man's entrance into his sadness can start with his consciously observing his body, recognizing that feeling in the chest or gut and then being open to honor it in whatever way feels right.

This is not an easy task for men. An African tribe, the Gusli, has a ritual for the men during the mourning period which consists of the men facing the women of the tribe as the women are grieving, actively crying, wailing, and keening. The purpose of this ritual is for the men to be able to put themselves into the mood of grief. By facing them, watching them, and listening to them, the men start to make a connection to their own bodies and their grief within. Even these tribal men have difficulty in putting themselves into the state of mind/body we are calling grief, but they have found a creative way to get around it.

The Potlatch Ceremony

The potlatch ceremony is a good example of men using their body to connect with their sadness. In the Athabaskan tribe of northwest North America, men dance out their feelings by singing "sorry songs." The ceremony is attended by both men and women, and the men usually start the ritual by drumming. After the drumming starts, the singing begins. The first song is usually a "sorry song" about the person who has just died. Sorry songs are often sung in a slow rhythmic monotone, the words creating images of the deceased, a lament for their absence, and describing the associated feelings of loneliness and loss. The singers sway rhythmically to the beat of the song as they take short shuffling steps. By coupling the swaying movement of the body with the words and songs about the deceased, a man can connect his grief with his body. During the first song, the bereaved family comes onto the dance floor and is encircled by the other participants. They sing to and *physically* support the family, as the sorry song brings out the grief of the family and others. Gradually the sorry songs are sung not only about this most recent death, but also about other people who have died in the past. The potlatch becomes a container for the grief of the community as a whole, not just the presently bereaved family. As the evening goes on, the drummers begin to alternate the sorry songs with "dance songs," uplifting and faster paced songs that are designed to shift the mood gradually away from grief and into a more joyous spirit. It is said that the dancers used to dance and sing these songs for days on end, but now the duration is limited to the potlatch length of three days.[12]

We have no grief rituals in our culture like the potlatch. Given this deficit, and all of the restrictions men experience on acknowledging and expressing their sadness during grief, it is not surprising that it is an uncommon public experience. It is going to take a warrior-like effort on the part of men to bring about changes related to their expression of sadness. As men we are challenged with a tough situation, in some ways opposite to the position women found themselves in prior to the "women's movement." The women were challenged to develop their outer selves, i.e. in the workplace. One of the challenges we face as men is to use our strengths in order to develop our feeling side. If we can work with our sadness, there can be an abundance of benefits, as Chogyam Trungpa reminds us in "The Myth of Freedom": "Tenderness contains an element of sadness. It is not the sadness of feeling sorry for yourself or feeling deprived, but it is a natural situation of fullness. You feel so full and rich, as if you were about to shed tears. Your eyes are full of tears, and the moment you blink, the tears will spill out of your eyes and roll down your cheeks. In order to be a good warrior, one has to feel this sad and tender heart. If a person does not feel alone and sad he cannot be a warrior at all."[13]

Guilt

In tribal cultures, when a chief died there was often a search for the responsible party. In their consciousness they had a need to find the perpetrator of such an injustice as to cause the death of their chief. We may make fun of this "primitive" process, but it appears to continue today in the form of guilt. The search has been sidetracked and is now turned back on the self. People who experience a significant grief will usually experience some form of guilt. The guilt is characterized by searching for the responsibilities we did or did not take prior to the death. It usually takes the form of shoulds and shouldn'ts. A common example is "I should have called him before he died; we hadn't talked in a month" or " I shouldn't have gone on that outing. I could have been there when he died."

The intensity of this process varies considerably depending on many factors. One of these factors is the circumstances of the death. In the death of a child there is almost always a good deal of guilt. Fathers feel, even if it is not justified, that they were responsible for the safety of their children. When the child dies, no matter what the circumstances might be, the father will usually feel a significant amount of guilt. Our frame of reference has narrowed so that what at one time was a community-wide sense of responsibility is now laid completely at our own feet. The family has become the equivalent of the tribe, and many times the man feels responsible, as if he were the chief. The irrational idea that underlies most guilt in grief is "Men are the tribal chiefs of their family, and I have failed in my task to protect my tribe." This is a difficult state of mind and needs to be brought out into the open in order for it to be healed. Men I have worked with have been helped a great deal by checking out this intense sense of responsibility with other men, or with women. Don't hunt yourself down in a lethal chase with guilt. If you do, you are positioning yourself for paralysis.

Guilt and Kings

Another analog to guilt in grief is the role of kings. In ancient cultures where the king was nearing divine status, the people connected all that happened to them with the presence of the king. If all was well, then the king was wonderful. If there was continued drought, the king was many times held responsible for this. The end product of some of these scenarios was the killing of the king in order to bring about change in the kingdom. Bad times, it must be a bad king, kill him. This is another outer example that may reflect our inner guilt. We start to see a part of ourselves as the "bad king." Sometimes the guilt becomes so intense that there are suicidal feelings on the part of the man who is grieving. In fact, thoughts of suicide are a frequent result of grief, although many people don't talk about them. There can be a sense of wanting to join the person who has died, or there can be a complete loss of wanting to continue living. The feelings that follow intense guilt in grief include inadequacy and unworthiness, to the point of feeling that you are not worthy of continuing to live. In that case, the suicidality is a result of seeing yourself as the bad king and wanting to take him out.

Guilt is a Type of Thinking

Guilt is somewhat different from the other feelings of grief. We need to differentiate the guilt we are speaking of from other forms of guilt, particularly the guilt that has a productive message for us. For instance, maybe our guilt over drinking and driving and causing an accident has an important message for us about our need to change that behavior. In the typical guilt of grief, many people don't think that guilt is a feeling at all. They see it more as a process of thinking, comprised of negative self-thoughts. I have found this to be true in my practice.

One method for dealing with guilt can be found in the sentence "Guilt is putting today's knowledge on yesterday's problems." Most of the irrational guilt that stems from grief can be summarized with this sentence. People tend to forget that they did not know at the time of death or whenever, what they now know. A common example of this is the sense that many men get of feeling guilty about not connecting with the person who died just prior to their death. Men can sometimes carry around a profound self-judgment about not making this particular last contact. What most of these men have forgotten is that they did not know the hour of death, and if they had, they would have made the contact.

Another example is a man whose son died in a car accident. The accident was caused by a 16-year-old girl who was drinking and driving. This man felt a great deal of guilt over not providing his son with a car that would have given him more protection, a big boat of a car. He felt that as his responsibility in the accident. He felt he should have made certain that the automobile his son was driving could have protected him from harm. He did not consider that the son really liked the car he drove and didn't want a big boat of a car. Had this man known that his son was going to be in such an accident, he would have bought him *anything* he could to protect him, but he didn't know. This is the way it is with guilt in grief. We need to avoid putting today's knowledge on yesterday's problems.

Helplessness

Men frequently will enter a grieving process with the same energy they have found successful in dealing with other types of problems. For many men, this is a process of saying "I can handle this, I'll push my way through this, I'm powerful enough." We have a certain pride in our physical strength, and sometimes generalize this strength to the emotional realms. We try the active and powerful methods of problem solving we may have used with other problems, and it doesn't seem to put a dent in the grief. We try the next day and get the same result. We try and try and the grief seems unaffected. Then comes the sense of helplessness and powerlessness. Not only are we powerless in the face of death, we also now are seemingly powerless in the face of this thing called grief. No one has told us that this might last a long time. This sense of powerlessness is one of the most difficult aspects of grief for men. It conflicts with our sense of mastery and power. Grief is a problem without a solution, and this is extremely frustrating for men who value their problem-solving capacities.

Protecting the Garden

Men need to know that grief can last a long time, that it is not a short-term endeavor. We also need to know that the usual methods of change that we use on the outer world are not effective when it comes to working with the inner world of grief. Trying to "push" grief is like being in a deep pool of water and trying to "push" the water. The more you push, the more the water seems to flow back into the space you just pushed it from. What those usual methods can do is put us into position to work with the inner world. Robert Moore talks of the "warrior" energy needing to protect the lover energy while the lover is in "the garden.[14]" When Moore speaks of the warrior he is speaking of the part of ourselves that takes action. When speaking of the lover he is describing the part that is capable of merging with whatever feeling is present. What he is talking about is the need for the active part to protect the part that enjoys. Think about the number of times you might have been interrupted by some responsibility when trying to enjoy yourself. Telephone calls, beepers, salesmen, a project that keeps you from going with your family to an outing, all of these are examples where our enjoyment was interrupted by one thing or another. This is an example of the warrior part of ourselves not "protecting the garden," thus leaving ourselves unable to obtain the joy available from the garden. The interesting thing is that this lover part is not only the part that is able to enjoy, it also is the part that is able to merge with the grief. Men tend to need their activity (warrior) to put themselves into a safe place to experience the grief they are feeling. We need our active parts to put us in a position to experience, honor, and acknowledge our grief.

It has been my experience that when men are successful in providing this kind of space, and in standing in their tension of their pain, that they are very efficient in working with the feelings that emerge. It is a matter of the outer warrior being able to learn to transform his outer skills and use them on the inner world of grief and feelings. The whole process is an exercise in learning to stand your ground, not only outside in the world, but inside within your psyche.

6

Gender Differences

We are beginning to understand gender differences relating to the way men and women communicate. This information has been popularized by Deborah Tannen's book *You Just Don't Understand.*[15] This information is fascinating, but it doesn't go quite far enough. While it is informative about the communication differences, it doesn't explain the difference in a man and woman's nature in processing emotions. This chapter will examine some of the findings of gender difference research and then take that extra step to theorize how these differences affect men and women in their grieving.

Physical Differences

The underlying nature of men and women is different in many ways. A good place to start are the physical differences. It has been recently theorized that the hormone prolactin is related to a man's having less access to the use of emotional tears.[16] Prolactin is a hormone that is instrumental in emotional tear production. It seems that levels of prolactin drop at about the time a young boy enters adolescence. It is theorized that this drop makes it more difficult for boys (and later men) to access emotional tears. This physical difference tells us that a man will be less likely to access his tears in grief due in some part to physiological reasons. I can remember the distance I had from emotional tears as an adolescent. I can now understand this in a different way, knowing that a part of that change was probably physiological. This difference can be seen around the world in various cultures and is not limited to North America. Men tend to cry less following a loss.

Another physical difference is provided by research which indicates that men and women have significant differences in brain structure. One of these differences was reported in *Time* magazine in an article which described the corpus callosum as thicker in women's brains than in men's.[17] The corpus callosum is a structure that connects the two hemispheres of the brain. One hypothesis theorizes that this difference gives a woman a greater connection between her verbal capacity and her feelings, and leaves a man less able to verbalize feeling states. If this hypothesis is true, it would help explain why men tend toward activity in engaging their grief. It would also help us in understanding the perennial problem in relationships where women are left baffled about why their men don't talk as freely as they do about their feelings. If you listen to a man talking about his grief, he will generally describe his grief not in terms of feelings but in terms of his own body, i.e., a heaviness in the chest or stomach. We will see in this section how a man's activity connects him to his body and to his feelings.

Psychological Differences

One important difference in men and women on a psychological level has to do with a man's need for autonomy. It stems from many factors, one of which is the difficult separation a boy experiences from his mother at about age four. At that time the mother feels that it is no longer appropriate for the young boy to have "unlimited access" to her body, which he had when he was an infant and probably a toddler. He is told not to touch certain parts and is not allowed to enter the bathroom when his mother is there, even though he sees his sisters doing so. This is the initial separation which young boys experience, a pulling away of the mother from the son, which the young girls don't have to go through. The young boy learns how to be autonomous and to alternate between periods of autonomy and periods of intimacy. This pattern continues in his relationships as an adult male where he tends to move back and forth with his partner from intimacy to autonomy.[18] The man needs periods away from his spouse in order to be ready to approach his spouse for intimacy. This pattern also can be seen in the way a man grieves. Men will tend to move in and out of their grief, finding things, places, or activities to serve as mechanisms for this movement.

Men and the Hierarchy

Men tend towards a hierarchical nature, viewing the world in terms of who is governing whom. Women, on the other hand, tend to view the world through the lens of who is relating to whom. Tannen points out that men live in a hierarchical world that is characterized by having the consciousness of who is "one up" or "one down." Conversations are seen by men as a place to maintain their image and to avoid being put into a one down position, with the goal of maintaining their independence. It is easy to see this developing in boys as they learn in grade school to put each other down. A great deal of effort and energy goes into creating and remembering put downs in order to be ready for the word battle that goes on between boys. This is the beginning of hierarchy. It can also be seen in the knowledge that each young boy has about who in his class can kick the farthest, run the fastest, etc. The hoped for goal of the boy and later the man is to appear to be on top of things and, above all, maintain independence.

Women, however, tend to live in a network of support. Their concern is not so much to appear independent but to seek connection with their peers, not from a hierarchical standpoint but from a position of being equal. Their negotiations are more for closeness, both seeking and giving confirmations of support, rather than maintaining status. The keyword for women is "intimacy," which is a measure of the degree that women are related to each other. Men have a keyword of "independence." The object of their striving in the hierarchy is to maintain and enhance their independence and position.

Hierarchy

To understand a man's hierarchical nature we need to know what this thing called hierarchy is and how it came to be. Many people have theorized about the origins of the hierarchy. One explanation looks at the hunter/gatherer roles that have been our ancestry. The men were those who usually hunted. In order to hunt they needed to depend on each other. A part of this dependence was the hunters capacity to be quiet and to communicate to one another without making a commotion. One can imagine a group of men hunting together using hand signals to express the complex movements and actions needed to stalk and kill the prey. There was a need for an identified leader, someone who would decide when and where to act. The hunt was no place for a group decision or gathering the thoughts and feelings of others before coming to a decision. Thus, there must have been some hierarchical strata that aided the men in working together. They needed to be quiet and follow the directions of one man who lead. If that man was killed during the hunt, there was probably a man already designated to take over his role, and a third and a fourth. We can see the need for this type of hierarchy given the situation the men faced.

This can be contrasted with the gatherer roles that women tended to enact. In gathering the needed foods, women many times worked in groups to gather or to clean and make preparations. It is easy to imagine groups of women talking and communicating with each other as they completed their tasks together. This type of activity also lends itself to group decisions and deciding together what to do, rather than having to depend on a specific woman for leadership and direction.

Some interesting gender differences can be linked to this hierarchy/ relational schema. Men are known to have better skills at mentally rotating three dimensional objects in space. Some theorize that this is due to the thousands of years men spent hunting, where their lives were dependent on visually tracking three dimensional objects. A man also throws and runs differently than a woman. These skills also seem related to our ancestry of hunting. Men had to pursue prey and throw spears in the hunt. Over the years the men who threw well and ran quickly were more likely to survive and have children.

With these histories it is easy to assume that the men were more practiced at stealth, strength, and quiet within a hierarchical network while the women tended to be more relational and democratic with each other during their work. The men relied on a designated hierarchy while the women probably had more of the luxury of deciding together what they would do. While in their village, the men were probably responsible for providing for the community and protecting the rest of the group. The expectation must have been that the man would sacrifice his safety for the safety of others.

Hierarchy at Work and Play

It is easy to see how these ideas can play out in a man's work. Fire fighting, for example, has long been a male-dominated profession, and maybe the above ideas have something to do with that. A fireman expects to put himself at great physical risk as he performs his job of protecting the community. He does this within a hierarchy designated by rank. Similarly, policeman put themselves at risk to protect their community, also within a hierarchy of rank. With both of these professions it is easy to see the similarity to the hunters of old, putting themselves at risk for the safety of their community, designated to provide, protect, and sacrifice. It is interesting that the men who are involved in this sort of work tend to report that they easily bond with the men with whom they work.

We find the same process in the armed forces. Men are in a hierarchy with the goal of protecting the community. They are stratified by a complex system of rank, and the hierarchy of the organization is reflected in all that goes on. The chain of command is a sacred issue, with men honoring the rank above them with respect and obedience.

The construction business offers another example. One only has to observe a construction site for a short time to see how the men work together. There is remarkably little interaction or talking. Much of the time hand signals and gestures get the point across as these men work together under the direction of the foreman.

The same hierarchical ideas tend to also dominate a man's play. Think of a baseball or a football team. Signals pass between the pitcher and the catcher, and the quarterback signals changes in the play at the line of scrimmage. Also note the hierarchy and leadership on a sports team. As the team goes into a huddle it is only one man who gives the next play; the entire team follows along, rarely speaking out against the call.

Competition of all kinds is related to the hierarchy. Competition is merely a means of placing oneself in the hierarchy, a result of the desire to be one or more rungs higher on that ladder. Whether it involves a trout fishing tournament, the Super Bowl, or your job at the office, competition is a ritual which most men have played out repeatedly. A boyhood example of this is choosing sides for a ball game. Someone always has to be first and last in the order of choosing. It is often a painful identification of where you stand on the ladder, how high or low you are in the eyes of your peers. I can remember the relief I would feel as a boy if I could maneuver myself into a position of choosing the sides rather than being chosen. In this way the pain of being chosen in the middle or near the end was avoided. It is hard to imagine little girls choosing sides to play house.

Hierarchy is also present in relationships. Men, having become sensitized to hierarchical arrangements, can easily misinterpret requests as being "ordered around" by their wife. I have seen this cause trouble repeatedly in relationships. The wife will ask the man to do something for her, and he, feeling she is not asking but commanding, will respond in a negative fashion. He many times is feeling as if his wife assumes that she is above him on the hierarchy. The woman is unaware of the dilemma and assumes that the man just doesn't care about her. Both the man and the woman end up feeling hurt by this.

Gender and Healing

What does all this have to do with grief? These basic differences lead to dramatically different strengths and paths in processing emotions and, therefore, in the way men and women grieve. Both men and women are affected by our cultural avoidance of death and grief, but this avoidance has a different effect on the two sexes. A woman generally has an easier time in dealing with this prohibition in that she probably has a system of support in place in which intimacy is the keyword. This network of friends or family will often encourage the sharing of grief as a means to connect and therefore become more intimate. A man many times has no such system. He highly values independence and autonomy and sharing grief could be a threat to that. By revealing his grief to another man, he would be putting himself one or more rungs down on the hierarchy. The hierarchy values action and what can be done about things, not emotional connection. It is interested in product, efficiency, action, and outcome.

For a man to share his grief, he needs to know that he is respected. For a woman to share her grief, she needs to know that she will be related to. The reason for this need for respect is the result of the hierarchy: in the hierarchy respect is a keyword and is intimately related to one's position on it. This can be easily observed in groups of men who are healing their grief. The work of talking about their grief is usually put off until the men know that they have the respect of the other men. The men tend to naturally avoid talking about their grief for another reason. They see their grief as a burden and don't want to lay that on anybody. In the hierarchical arrangement where product and output are of importance, grief is seen as an impediment to product and output and is therefore not something men want to "share" with others. This can be contrasted with the woman's more natural fit with grief being connected with her leaning towards increasing intimacy. Men see grief as being something that is a problem and a burden, and within an hierarchy you don't place a burden on someone who has no responsibility for it. To express this to another man or to a woman would be, firstly, an admission that he was unable to handle his problems by himself (a sign of a lack of independence) and secondly, a dumping of a negative pile of stuff onto someone else who had no responsibility for it.

Using Action to Heal Grief

So what do men do with their grief? We have found that men tend to value autonomy, independence, and action. We have also found that men are less efficient in processing feelings verbally. How do men deal with their grief? They use their strengths of action. Action is valued in the hierarchy, and men use this as a catalyst to their grief. This action usually provides a place or thing and something to do with their bodies. A simple example is the activity of looking at a family picture album. Many men use this activity as a means of entering their grief. It is an action with a beginning and an end; you pick up the book and when finished put it back on the shelf. This beginning and end help to mark the boundaries of the experience for a man. Bill's wife had died six months prior, and sometimes after he got the kids to bed he would take out the picture album. He would sit in his chair while leafing through the book. His tears would flow as he looked at the various pictures. It was this *action* (as opposed to *interaction* for women) that helped Bill put himself into the space of grief, becoming more aware of his memories and his body's reaction to the loss.

Another example of how this works is a man whose high school-age son died in a car accident. In the first month or two after the death the man started to put together a book about his son. This was not a book that he intended to publish, but basically a book of memories. He did this by coordinating many of his son's friends and teachers in bringing this *product* about. Many hours were spent working together, gathering items that would become a part of the book, planning and talking about what should go into it. Teachers were involved in the process, and the young man's coaches, ministers, girlfriends, and ex-girlfriends. It was a community affair, and during this process this man spent a great deal of time talking with others about his son's life and listening to the stories others had to tell. This interaction was very similar to what might have happened had the man gone into a therapy group, but it was different in some significant aspects. All of his interactions were connected with a product—the book. He was the editor and producer of this product, and in this way he maintained his independence. His interactions with others relating to his son's death were connected to the production of this book, but they were no less healing than someone who chose to relate their grief to another person without the accompanying action. The man found healing for his grief through action that was harmonious with his need for independence and his orientation towards producing a product.

When looking at a man's grief from this perspective, it is easier to see why men tend to grieve in a private and quiet manner. They don't want to be a burden to others, they want to maintain their independence, and they want to use their strength of action in dealing with a very powerful force such as grief. Much has been written about the pathology of a man's tendency to grieve alone but when seen in this vein it can be understood as a personal choice the man makes rather than a step into pathology.

The fact is men and women grieve differently. Following the death of a child, for instance, a mother will grieve by crying and talking with her close friends and family. The father, more hierarchical in nature, is more inclined to relate to events through physical action rather than feelings. The grieving father may perform some sort of action such as creating a book, starting a scholarship in the name of the child, or raising money for a special interest the child had. He will want to *do* something to connect with his grief.

This difference many times leads to misunderstandings. Men and women tend to be suspicious about the other's mode of grief. He may think that she is "overdoing it" as she emotes in the presence of those close to her. She may feel that the man is not really grieving because he grieves in private or through action, not sharing his tears in the same way she does. Yet both styles need to be honored because both, when used effectively, accomplish the same goal— coming to terms with the loss.

It is important to note that the use of action in healing grief is not exclusive to men; some women use action-oriented healing and use it well. In the same vein, many men are able to use relational skills to heal their grief. When a man relates his grief to others, particularly to men, it can be a powerful healing. We are painting with broad strokes when we attempt to link men with action and women with relating. In general, men tend towards action as a primary mode in healing their grief while using relating as a secondary mode, and women are the opposite. A man's action can serve as a ritual container for grief *if* he forms a conscious link between the action and the loss. Each time he performs the action it activates the grieving process and moves it toward healing. Men honor and acknowledge their grief by connecting it to their actions and preparing a specific place that allows the grief to emerge.

7

Healing Through Action:
The Masculine Gift

The feelings of sadness, anger, helplessness, and guilt comprise the bulk of grief. The healing of these feelings is accomplished by processing the grief a bit at a time, using ritual. Many people believe that the healing of grief is only accomplished through crying and talking about it. While this is probably the most efficient means, there are many others. This chapter is about these "other" forms of healing grief. It is these modes that we are calling the masculine gift of healing. Women tend to feel safe in talking about their grief with others; men for many reasons don't tend to see "sharing" grief in this way as particularly safe. Men tend to find more safety in realms where they feel more comfortable: their actions. These active rituals, or "other" forms of healing grief, perform the same function as crying and talking about one's grief. They provide a safe place to immerse oneself a bit at a time in the chaos of the grief. This immersion is characterized by honoring and acknowledging the pain within. By talking about it, we are acknowledging and also honoring the presence of the grief. By having another person listen, we are spreading the grief even farther. Being heard by another tends to quicken the process of healing and also to lessen any shame that may be a part of one's grief. Crying and talking about one's grief are extremely effective means in healing grief, but there are as many ways to honor and acknowledge our grief as there are people who grieve. We will examine some of those different ways to grieve, ways of healing that vary from the norm of crying and talking about it, but are effective tools for the healing of grief.

The following gives numerous examples of the ways men have found actions, places, or things to help them in connecting with their pain. A man's action can serve as a healing container for grief *if* he forms a conscious link between the action and the loss. Each time he performs the action, it activates the grieving process and moves it toward healing. The important aspects are that you do it consciously (do it intentionally, not let it happen to you), and that you in some way honor and acknowledge your grief in the process. Connecting the grief to one's activities has a similar effect as talking about it. They are both simply a means to experience the pain a bit at a time. The first section focuses on creativity, the second on practicality, and the third on thinking. These three categories of actions are only important in that they give us a way to sub-divide different actions a man might take in connecting to his grief. The importance is in the action, not into which category it fits .

Creativity

A man I know told me of his memories as a young boy of his father's reaction to his mother's death. Shortly after his mother died, his father bought a large block of wood and placed it on the dining room table. Over the next two or three years, the father sculpted a bust of his dead wife. Each time he approached the wood and began carving, this creative action brought him in touch with his grief for his wife. It was also a reminder to the children of their mother and their father's love and grief for her. Through his creative action this man slowly healed his grief.

Grief expressed through creative action is one mode of the masculine gift of healing. In this mode, people tend to use creative efforts— works of art, poetry, or music—to acknowledge and honor their grief. For example, I know a man who created special Christmas cards commemorating his wife's death in a previous year. Through this activity he was able to honor and acknowledge his own loss and share it with his community of friends and family. The process of making and sending the cards was a mechanism for this man to experience his grief. Eric Clapton's hit single "Tears in Heaven" is another example of a man's linking his creativity to his grief. This song is in memory of his four year-old son who died in an accident. Lou Reed's album "Magic and Loss" expresses his grief for two friends who died in a period of a year. Reed used his creative activity to connect with his grief within. Sometimes a man's grief is brought to the surface by listening to music or by reading poetry. Abraham Lincoln had a male friend who would come to the White House at his request and sing what Lincoln called "sad songs." During these *activities* Lincoln would sit quietly and cry. He was using the creative element to contact his grief.

Another example of grieving through creativity is the quilt created to honor those who have died from AIDS. This is a beautiful example of creative action as a focal point for grief. Those who see the quilt are struck by the personal nature of each panel. The planning and creating of each section requires creative action. In doing this they are using their action to create a place to act as a catalyst for their feelings. When displayed, the quilt also provides a contained space for the expression of grief, through which men and women can walk as they honor their grief. There are many additional examples of men using their creativity to honor and acknowledge their grief, including symphonies, poems, and paintings.

Practicality

A man who uses his practicality in his grieving acknowledges and expresses his feeling of loss in a physical, tangible way. His grief takes on a practical and sensate quality. In the practical mode, men will tend to do things in *honor of the loss*. I worked with one man whose son was killed in a car accident. To deal with his grief the man got involved in a victim's rights group, donating his time and skills as a lawyer. In *doing* this he found a contained place where he could freely communicate his thoughts and feelings about his grief. He was able to tell his story over and over as someone else might do in a therapy group, but he did it as a part of his service *activity*. Not only does such service work join the man's activity with his grief, it also has the potential to imbue the death with meaning. Grief without meaning can be a dangerous and prolonged experience.

Dedicating One's Work

Another example of this mode occurs when people dedicate work in honor of someone who has died or been injured. The Detroit Lions recently dedicated their season to a player who had been paralyzed. In this way the players transformed their arena into a space that could be used to express their grief for their injured teammate.

Nolan Richardson, the head coach of the Arkansas national championship basketball team, was asked after the final game about his daughter who had died some years prior. Richardson replied that after each game won, as he walked out of the arena, he said to her, "Baby, we got you another one." This statement tells us that Richardson had connected his grief for his daughter with his greatest skill, being a basketball coach. One can easily imagine how Richardson thought of his daughter during each game, and even each practice, and had dedicated his work in her memory.

Creating Memorials

A man who had two family members killed in a car accident on a highway near his home developed his own ritual to deal with this tragedy. Near the spot where the accident occurred, he erected two wooden crosses that he had made and painted white. These homemade markers violated local codes, and so the police would come and take them down. Shortly thereafter the man would go through his ritual all over again. Each time he made and erected crosses he gave himself the opportunity to connect his grief with his action. This behavior typifies grieving through practicality. All memorial structures are classic examples of this type of grieving. Buildings and statues have been designed and built by men for millennia to commemorate the deceased. The Taj Mahal is just one example, and Washington D.C. with all of its memorials is another.

One man I know who is retired dedicates his early morning routine to his wife who died a year before. When he gets up and gets his coffee, he sits at the breakfast table and speaks with his wife as if she were there. His conversations become a place in which he re-connects with his wife and experiences the pain of her death. A man whose daughter died has conversations with her in his car as he is driving. The man and his daughter used to converse as he was driving her to school, and now he has created an activity of talking with her as he drives. By doing this he is putting himself into a space that honors and acknowledges his grief for his daughter. He has connected his driving and his memories of his daughter in the car and has found a way to honor and acknowledge her, and his feelings.

Another man whose daughter died found a way to connect to his grief by taking a ring which had belonged to his daughter and wearing it. Each time he notices her ring on his finger he remembers his connection to her and his related grief. It has become a reminder to him of his daughter and a catalyst for his feelings.

Using Special Interests

Another path into grief is to think of the special interests of the person who died. Bert Hoff, a friend of mine from Seattle, experienced the death of his father,[19] a "mountain man" type who spent a great deal of time in the surrounding mountainous regions of Seattle. There was one particular place that the father loved dearly. After his father's death, Bert took his father's ashes to that place and had a private funeral ceremony. He spread his fathers ashes there and has since connected his feelings of grief for his father with this place. Each time he visits or thinks of that place he thinks of his father and his grief. There are as many different ways to do this as there are people. You need to find the best way for you.

Rituals can be created out of almost any activity. It is not the importance of the type of activity that concerns us, but the connection of our pain and grief with that activity. Families can create activities that honor the person who has died. For instance, a family I know of decided to leave an empty place setting at their dinner table in honor of the member of their family who died. Another family decided to continue to give presents from the person who had died to its members. The mother bought and wrapped the presents and labeled them from the father prior to giving them to the teen-age children. Activities such as these will not work for every family. Each family needs to create their own grief rituals that will be right for them, but they are examples of how some families have connected to their grief through an active ritual.

Bringing ritual into your grief is intended to connect a place, thing, or activity with your grief. The actions of my friend in Seattle are a good example of using a place, the man wearing his daughter's ring is an example of using a thing, and the man who made the white crosses an example of an activity.

Gardening

If you have a strength in gardening this is a good place to make an earthy connection with your grief. My own perennial garden in my back yard is at the edge of some woods. It has served me well in connecting with my grief. As people I have known have died, plants in my garden have represented that person to me. An example was a mentor of mine who died suddenly of a heart attack. This was an older man, a minister, who had been a boyhood friend of my father's. This man's friendship had meant a great deal to me. The day he died, I found out that the shipment to me of a water plant, a lotus, was canceled. Three days later the lotus mysteriously appeared in the mail. Then a few days after that another lotus arrived. I called the nursery and explained that they had mistakenly sent two of these beautiful plants. They told me that it was their mistake and to keep them both and enjoy them. Ever since then I have connected my friend John with both of those plants. When I go out and sit next to the water garden and admire the giant lotus leaves and flowers it always connects me with John and my grief.

Another incident in my garden happened the day I read Earthman's last column in the *Washington Post*. Earthman was the gardening columnist whose columns I always looked forward to reading. He was a practical, down-to-earth fellow who had a love of gardening and a deep concern for the earth. He was outspoken about avoiding the use of any chemicals in the garden. His columns were as much about his own growth as those of the garden. When I read his last column which explained at the bottom that he had died the week prior, I was saddened. In that column he said a particular plant, the arum, is now up. When I read this I said to myself, "No it is not, not mine." When I checked in my garden, sure enough there it was plain as day. Ever since then that plant, the arum, has represented this man and his death to me. Every time I notice my arum, I think of the Earthman, his life and writing, and my grief for him.

Another ritual which can be used in the garden is the ritual of the Cree Indians of northwest North America. I have summarized the ritual as follows:

When his brother died suddenly, Jaque was torn by sadness and anger. Following ancient custom, he went into the forest, selected a tree and, after uttering a prayer, stripped away a piece of the bark. Now the tree, like Jaque, had lost something whose loss caused deep pain. Many times over the following months he returned to visit the tree. As the seasons passed, the wound in the tree healed. So did the wound in Jaque's heart. With the tree as a visible reflection of his loss, Jaque was reminded that he, too, was healing.

This ritual incorporates many elements of which we have been speaking. It provides an action in cutting the tree, a thing (the tree and its wound), and a place to visit to reconnect with our pain and healing. The power of this ritual is difficult to express through writing. I urge you to try it yourself and experience the healing that can follow.

Thinking

The thinking function offers another mode for connecting with grief. However, this is probably the most difficult because it is the opposite of the feeling function, the obvious home of grief. The thinking function is a cerebral element; logic, not feeling, is at home here. A person who grieves through this function will choose *activities* involving thought processes.

Meditation

An obvious method for working with grief through the thinking function is meditation. If a man meditates daily, he is consciously putting himself into ritual, and contained space. By turning his attention inward and slowing down his pace, he becomes more open and receptive to his inner world. This process allows the contents of the psyche to arise and be dealt with. Meditation is better known as being the search for the "Inner King," but the path towards that goal must pass through our own personal stuff, including our grief. By meditating a man is using his thinking function as an action to contact his grief.

Letter Writing

Letter writing is an activity that can help us in approaching our grief in a straightforward manner. It is a very simple task that you can work with to help you in connecting with your grief. You simply write a letter to the person who died. This is not a letter intended to be mailed, but one that carries the sole purpose of creating a space within which you can stand in the tension of your own grief. I have found in working with people and letter writing that the information, thoughts, feelings, and ideas that arise during this exercise many times are significantly different from our everyday thoughts. It seems that writing something down somehow puts us in touch with a different part of our brain, and new material tends to arise. You can write a letter to a person who has died or you can write a letter to a job you lost. The addressee makes no difference; the important part is to consciously direct your attention to your inner experience of the loss.

Active Imagination

Active imagination is another way to stand in one's tension of grief that is especially helpful to men who have strong analytical skills. It is a way to talk to the various parts of yourself. Most people don't think that they are a "plurality," but when you think about it, it is certainly true. We have a persona which we have already mentioned, and a part that becomes moody when we avoid our grief, plus various other parts. It is possible to connect to these various parts by using a method called active imagination. You simply take out a clean sheet of paper, find a quiet place, and write a question to any part of yourself, in this instance to your grief. A good question to start with might be something like, "Grief, what do I need to know about you?" After you have written the question on the paper, you put the pencil down and listen for the first response that comes into your mind. No matter what that response is, write it down. Then you proceed to respond to that with your next question. In this way you create a dialogue within yourself. Sometimes what comes into your mind will seem like garbage. If the first thing that came to mind was "a bag of French fries," then you respond to that with your next written question. For instance, "Wait a minute, grief, I asked you a serious question. I want an answer. What do I need to know about you?" Then you put the pencil down and listen, and again write down the first thing that comes to your mind. You may have to sift through some garbage to get somewhere, but the chance of some worthwhile material springing forth is very good.

One of the questions I would highly recommend is to ask the grief what its name is. A name will spring into your mind and from that point onward you will have a name for your grief. This seems a little silly but it is very helpful. Having a name for the grief gives you a bit of a handle. The name many times will act as a symbol for the grief that is within. Examine closely the name that comes up. Who do you know by that name? Does that person give you any clue about your grief? What does the name mean to you? Many times the name that is offered to us is not understood at first. One time when I was doing this exercise a name for a part of myself came up that I didn't understand in the least. The name was Ptolemy. I was confused by this and didn't understand it's meaning until sometime later when I looked up Ptolemy and, among other things, found that he was the last man to believe that the earth was orbited by the sun. When I read this I laughed out loud. The name Ptolemy was the message I needed to hear. It fit precisely with the issue of my original question. It described my own arrogance in thinking that I was the center of the universe.

One man I know did this process and came up with "Fred" as the name for his grief. The name was helpful to him in many ways, one of which was that he would tell his wife, "Oh, oh, honey, I've got to go see Fred," and in this humorous vein he could alert her to his feeling state. If you approach this exercise in a serious, and open manner it will repay you by leading you to powerful new understandings of your inner workings. Entire books have been written on how to do active imagination. If you are interested in this kind of approach, seek out a good book. One example is a book called *Inner Work* by Robert Johnson,[20] half of which is devoted to teaching active imagination. The unconscious has parts that are interested in helping us heal and importantly, also has parts that want no such thing. Approach this exercise with caution; it is a powerful tool which is best used under the mentorship of one who has knowledge of its use.

Sometimes the grief is so strong that you might be tempted to avoid using any kind of ritual to connect with it. In the first year of a strong grief the feelings are powerful and need little encouragement to come forth. You need to be the judge as to when you might use some form of action as a means of connecting with it. As a general rule, even if the grief is strong and present, it is probably a good idea to connect it to some activity, place, or thing at that point. Each time you practice a conscious activity that connects you with your grief you are taking some of the pressure off the power of the grief. Many times it is an unnoticeable amount of pressure that is being released, but it is happening.

Ritual is important in the healing of grief. In our culture we have almost no rituals that are blessed and sanctioned for this healing. We are left to our own devices. It is an important part of our healing to find our own personal rituals and put them into place. It is critical that men find activities to connect them to their grief, for it is through some action, place, or thing that a man will be able to connect to his pain and slowly bring himself toward healing.

8

Our Own Culture

*I asked a man if people over the border, in Mali, spoke the
same tongue. He said, "No, but we understand them,
because they cut the prepuce of the boys as we do, and they
die our kind of death." Once a culture is deprived of its
death, it loses its health.*

Ivan Illich

Men and women have different ways to approach their
grief. These differences are affected by the culture in
which they live. A culture provides the ground to allow
the grief to grow and be healed. Our own culture provides fertile
soil for a variety of things, but not for grief. The "grief soil" of our
culture could be likened to a desert. The denial of death and grief
is massive, and this makes grieving difficult. How did we get to this
point in our attitudes toward death and dying? Let's have a look at
a few historical examples of the ways men and women dealt with
death and grief. We will follow this with a discussion about the
factors that have influenced our own culture and it's manner of
dealing with this issue.

The Middle Ages

A man sensed that he was dying. He alerted the people closest to him that this was happening and proceeded into the place where he slept. He readied himself and lay down upon his back on his bed, spreading his arms in the shape of a cross. People started streaming into the room. His family, relatives, children, neighbors, even people he didn't know who lived nearby, crowded into the small space. These people had been alerted to the process by seeing the priest carrying the *viaticum* through the streets. As they saw this, they felt a responsibility to attend the ritual that would follow and dropped what they were doing in order to attend. As the people gathered in the room, the windows and doors were shut and candles were lit. The man who was dying started the ritual process and controlled the timing of the event. He proceeded to say good-bye to those around him, and offered his apologies for deeds he had done that he felt needed forgiveness. He offered his forgiveness to those present. He proceeded to speak the ritual words that he had learned from attending this same ritual many times before as an observer. After he had finished, he lay in waiting for death to come.

This story is a description of the way men died in the Middle Ages. The deathbed experience was an intimate endeavor that was a part of one's community. Men (and women) had a sizable fear of sudden and unexpected death because it would rob them of this experience of their final ritual. There was a sense of pride that men had in being able to anticipate the time of their death. This was made somewhat easier by the lack of "good" medical care. Most major illnesses were fatal, and thus when someone became severely ill it usually meant that they were dying. This made it somewhat easier to predict with some accuracy the time of approaching death.

This information comes from a book by Philippe Aries entitled *Death in the Middle Ages.*[21] This book offers details about the attitudes of death and the way people dealt with it. He points out that the people of the Middle Ages were intimately connected with death. They tended to see it as a natural course and conclusion of their life on this earth. There was great importance placed on a man's knowing that he was about to die. Through outer signs or through intuitive inner knowing, the man became aware of his impending death and followed prescribed ritual and behavior.

Early America

Certainly the pioneers and colonists in our country were more closely related to death than we are today. Grief for them was more a matter of being a part of life. The customs and rituals these people used were simple and cost effective. They didn't have extra resources at hand for rituals of death and grief. This was a time when death was familiar to all. Children died at an alarming rate. In fact they used to have what were called "powder kids," the small children that were assigned the most dangerous job in the community, carrying the gunpowder. This was done because the children were the most expendable. If a male adult died, then many others would die as a result of his absence. It doesn't take a lot of thought to imagine the grief for a child killed by a gunpowder explosion.

As our country grew and resources became more plentiful the rituals around death and grief became more visible. In the Victorian era there were strict and rigid rules about grief and mourning. For a husband's death a wife was expected to grieve for two years, for the death of a parent or sibling the expectation was for one year, and for uncle, niece, aunt, or nephew the time was three months. The rules around clothing were rigid and strict and interestingly were applied more to women than to men. Clothing was to be black, with no shine in the fabric, and handkerchiefs were to be of cotton fabric with a black edging all around. The width of the band around the handkerchief was related to the time already spent in mourning; the thicker the black edge, the closer you were to the death.[22]

Clothing was not the only way that mourning was ritualized. After photographic equipment was available, it became popular to take pictures of the dead. The future president James A. Garfield hurried home from the Civil War to have his picture taken with his dead infant in his arms. Another president, Andrew Jackson, is said to have worn a gold locket around his neck in memory of his wife Rachel. Prior to cameras, people used artists to capture the images of those who were dying. There are stories of people calling artists to their death beds to capture their portrait just prior to their death.

I don't want to glorify the Victorian era because it was certainly lacking in many respects. One such area is that the cost involved in these ventures was awesome, and many aspects of the rituals were affordable only by a certain segment of the population. It also seems that this era focused on the external aspects a great deal, and I wonder how much of the internal work was being done.

Twentieth Century

As we moved out of the Victorian era and deeper into the twentieth century, we created increasing distance between ourselves and death. Death has moved out of the home and into funeral homes. We have developed a fascination with death from a distance through newspapers, TV, radio, and other media. How did we get where we are?

The answer begins with long term changes that have occurred over a number of centuries. In the Middle Ages people looked to the church for answers to their questions. Religion was a part of life, but the ones who held the answers were the leaders of the church and those answers were passed on to the pedestrian level in a parental sort of way. Gradually over time we moved out of looking to the church for answers and moved into a similar position with science. We look to science for our answers, but science has not been great in understanding death. Death is a mystery and does not lend itself to study. I can remember serving on an ethics committee of a local hospital and was amazed that there is quite a bit of scientific controversy over when a person is actually dead. In our culture today, if something hasn't been studied and proven by science it is not accepted. I have heard of a law in Georgia under which a person will be held liable for any statement about a product that cannot be proven by science and which negatively effects sales of the product. We have become dependent on science for our decisions in a way similar to the past dependence on the church in the Middle Ages.

One of the effects of science is the prolongation of life. People are living longer, and they are dying in hospitals rather than at home. This is also a major change. The locus of control over the deathbed experience has shifted out of the hands of the dying person as in the Middle Ages and into the hands of medical personnel. In the Middle Ages the majority of people died in their own surroundings. We can contrast this with the great majority of people who die in the hospital in this country. This has numerous effects, one of which is that it takes the control of the entire process out of the hands of the dying person and family and puts it into the hands of the medical community. During the Middle Ages the dying person would many times have a great deal of control over his environment and what happened there. The place of death also lent itself to continual support from both family and the community at large. It is worth pointing out that the hospice movement has begun to bring us back to having more control of our dying, but we have a long way to go.

This shift away from the community and into the invisible hospital has had a big effect on shaping our ideas of death and grief. We have lost touch with the body sensation of having death near to us. Grief is in many ways dependent on death as its father. Without a connection to death, grief becomes more of a mystery then it already is. It is my contention that this has had a significant effect on the way we grieve. As death has disappeared and our connection with it has been diminished, we are left with not really knowing in our body what we are grieving over.

Not only does this increase in longevity and technological expertise separate us even from death, it also has spun a myth in our culture that seems to loom just below consciousness—death is always preventable. As medical science increases its capacity to prolong life, this irrational belief seems to strengthen. One area that illustrates this myth of death as always being preventable is the flood of malpractice lawsuits in the courts. Ivan Illich has written about this problem and he states: "The witch hunt that was traditional at the death of a tribal chief is being modernized. For every premature or clinically unnecessary death, somebody or something can be found who irresponsibly delayed or prevented a medical intervention."[23]

Industrial Revolution

In the twentieth century the use of rituals started to slow down.

One of the reasons for this was the Industrial Revolution. With the advent of industrialization two things started to happen. One was the decay of the community as being a place of mutual support and dependence, and the other, the beginnings of the era of sub-contracting.

What is the difference between communities of today and those of our ancestors? In my mind, a major difference is that in our present day communities we are not dependent on our next door neighbor for our livelihood. Now we are dependent on our employer, who is usually some distance from our home. Our communities today are just groups of people who happen to live near each other and do their business someplace else. Men tend to bond and relate when there is a job to do, or if there is a threat. Most of our communities of today have neither. This is in contrast to the communities of the last century where men had responsibilities in the community and worked together to fulfill them. There were also situations that might arise in still older communities where the community was endangered in some way. The men of the community knew it was their responsibility to take action and through this activity became close with each other and their community. Examples of this type of bonding occur today in such professions as policeman or fireman or war-time bonding. A man today in a suburban subdivision is highly unlikely to feel bonded adequately to his neighborhood peers.

The second problem of the Industrial Revolution is sub-contracting. Since the middle of the last century we have been gradually dealing out all of our ritual responsibilities to professionals. From making a casket to the delivery of the oratory at the funeral, we have given out our death-related duties. Given them to funeral homes and funeral directors, doctors and medical professionals, florists and Hallmark.

This problem was further complicated by the effects of both World Wars. Many young men were killed in those conflicts, and many bodies never returned home. This intensified the problem of death being out of the locus of control and observation of the community.

Another effect of the industrial revolution was the absence of the father from the home. As Robert Bly has pointed out, this created a void in young boys not being able to be next to their father. Without being near him, the boys were less able to observe him or to literally feel his presence. They obviously were less likely to learn how to grieve.

As our culture has "progressed" we have also become a much more mobile society. This mobility is taking its toll on the depth of contact with the communities we have. We never know if someone is going to be here next year, or if they will be transferred on a moment's notice. This de-stabilizes what bonding we may have been able to create.

The nuclear dilemma is also related to our separation from death. Since the late fifties we have had the frightening reality that at any time the world come go up in flames. It reminds me in some ways of a tribal village that was always aware of the potential threat of annihilation from its neighbors and continually had to be on guard. One difference is that in the tribal setting the men could band together to try to protect their space. In our present day scenario, men don't have that same opportunity. We are left with a sense of helplessness, but also aware of the threat, be it conscious or unconscious awareness. I think that this nuclear threat is a part of the reason for our denial of death. It is too horrible to imagine, so we cut ourselves off from it. We just don't think about it. This separation from death can be seen in the fascination with death in the media. Violence and death are extremely popular subjects, as long as the death and violence are of the insulating type. By insulating I mean that the pain of the violence is rarely seen. The characters get back up again to fight in the sequel, or they were the bad guy and therefore don't count. We see a great deal of death on the screen, but rarely see the accompanying pain and grief.

Guerrilla Grief

Our culture is not a safe place to grieve. With the massive denial of death that occurs, there is a resulting disdain for grief. Both men and women are forced into a situation where their grief is not honored by the culture or the people around them. With our complete lack of grief rituals we have to practice what I call guerrilla grief. That is, grieving like a group might practice guerrilla warfare, outnumbered by the opposition, shooting from behind rocks, using hit and run tactics, and only coming out at night. One might say that the rocks are a little bit bigger for the women than they are for the men.

Our Desire and Our Grief

Our culture has the biggest per capita desire of any culture in the world. This leads necessarily to a great deal of grief. On the other hand, we set the record for the fewest rituals available to process grief. This is a dangerous position. We are left with a great deal of unfinished business, and no place to put it.

Our culture favors the happy, the material, the acquisition, the successful, and the new. Think back to our response to the Persian Gulf War. We emphasized the jubilant, the victorious, and the triumph of our high tech savvy. Not only did we not openly mourn for our own dead, we made plans to clandestinely bring back the dead bodies of our fighting men and have secret funerals. The message was grief is something that is not so important, and we had better hide it for national security reasons. Have we overlooked the grief for all of the Iraqis killed in this conflict? Men, women, and children killed, maimed, or made homeless, their homeland ripped to shreds. Did we hear anything about that? I didn't. What we saw were victory parades in the major cities and a display of our fighting power by filling the mall with military hardware and letting the children of our nation come and have their picture taken in front of an F-14. I am not against celebration, I just have a hard time with the one sidedness of our reaction.

Our culture is a death and grief denying culture. One writer on death and dying, Philippe Aries, has written that "the denial of death is openly acknowledged as a significant trait of our culture. The tears of the bereaved have become comparable to the excretions of the diseased." We whisk dead bodies through hospital corridors surreptitiously so no one will be offended by their presence, then paint them to make them look "lifelike."

I sometimes think that if our culture could be pictured as a human body, the resulting image would have a giant mouth and hands and a tiny colon. We purchase and consume tremendous amounts of material goods. It is odd that with this tremendous desire and gratification our culture is one of the weakest when it comes to grief. It seems that we are lopsided; our mouth and hands far outweigh our colon. The shadow side of our consumer culture is that we don't know what to do with our psychological "waste," i.e., our grief. One would expect a great deal of grief from all of this desire, but our culture doesn't honor it. Where does all that grief go? It goes underground and into our collective shadow. Just as an individual has a shadow side of things that are not conscious, our culture also has a shadow side, a part of which is grief. This can be seen by the names we call people when we don't like them, names like asshole or shithead. Many of the insults that we toss at those we don't like are related to waste and the end of our digestive tract. In my mind this parallels our cultural situation with grief.

Another impediment to our grief is the lack of role models. As a boy, how many men did you know who helped you in dealing with your grief? How did your father deal with grief? Have these models been of any help to you in contacting and releasing your old pain and loss? Your answer, I would guess, is no. We have very few role models out there of mature generative men dealing with their grief. We can compare this with Abraham Lincoln's reported open grieving in numerous situations. Lincoln apparently grieved with gusto even during his speeches, with flowing tears and moans of sorrow. Compare this to our culture of today. Can you imagine George Bush giving a speech and saying "I grieve for all of the women and children of Iraq who lost their homes, I grieve for all of the Iraqi soldiers who died in this conflict......." We don't see this.

Lack of the Numinous

Another reason for people being unrelated to their grief might be our distance from the numinous. By numinous I mean an experience that is highly charged with energy and mystery. The numinous is fuel for our body/soul engine, out there if only we can use our consciousness to contact it.

Two examples of numinous experiences are birth and death. Both illustrate how we have been insulated from the numinous in our culture. With birth, it is only recently that men have been allowed into delivery rooms. Women, of course, have been there all along, but even women have been insulated from the experience by the use of narcotizing medications. Think of death. We have allowed our culture to do quite a job in insulating us from the reality of death. Think of the last time you were in a funeral home. Were there rituals there that helped you in dealing with the death, or did you stand there uncomfortably not knowing what to say or talking with the guy next to you about the local sports team? There were no mourning songs for the men to sing together as is done in some cultures, no funeral drums to beat as is done in some cultures. There were no graves to dig or coffins to build; we pay people to do that. There were no rituals to perform. We have sub-contracted our way out of being next to death. Death in our culture is in many ways distanced from our senses, and when we find ourselves rubbing up against it we feel awkward and helpless, not knowing what to do or say.

When we touch the numinous we are not prepared for its power and usually will meekly follow the direction of the "professionals." Contrast this with the practices of the last century. Birth and death were more a part of the life of the community. Births took place at home, the children were involved, and the man had his responsibilities, preparing the space, fetching a mid-wife or doctor, keeping the fires burning, etc. Death also was a part of the home. Many times the body was laid out in the parlor (the name funeral parlor was chosen by the industry to remind people of their parlor at home) or some other room in the house. Can you feel the difference in distance from death and birth that we have brought on ourselves?

We are beginning to realize that distance and are taking steps to diminish it. Some innovative funeral homes and hospitals are helping people in experiencing the numinosity of death. One practice that is becoming more common is that of being with the body after the death occurs and sometimes washing the body. After the death the loved ones are encouraged to remain with the body and sit for a while. This is an opportunity to be in contact with the numinous. My own experience with sitting with the body has been that my appreciation of life becomes more clear. I can see myself as having a temporary body that wears out and dies. Knowing this, I treat my life in a different manner. Being in touch with death inevitably leads to being in touch with life.

9

Cross-Cultural Grief

Indigenous people around the world have highly developed rituals and mechanisms in place in their cultures to aid the resolution of grief. These rituals are an important part of life for these people. Their cultures are fertile ground for grief to be nourished. In many ways we are the primitives, because we have very few mechanisms in our culture that function in a similar way. By studying the way indigenous people grieve we can begin to get some idea about the state of grief in our own culture and our inadequate rituals. Using the analogy of a business or a sports team that is not doing well compared to the competition, we can examine a successful party and learn from their achievement. We will probably not adopt a specific grief ritual from another culture, but we will be able to see how these cultures have incorporated grief into their daily lives and how they have developed different rituals for men and women.

These cultures have implemented action-oriented rituals that allow both men and women tasks that connect them with their grief. In our own culture we have no such thing. We are left to our own devices to heal our grief, many times without the support of a caring community. Given this void of ritual, men and women are put into a precarious state. Often, women are able overcome this void by using their skills of relating and their natural tendency towards verbally sharing their grief with others, but men, usually with strengths of a different nature, are at more of a disadvantage. Without culturally-endorsed rituals men are left with nothing to *do* following a death. It has been my clinical observation that men in our culture grieve through task, that is, they find activities that allow them to access and heal their grief. Through studying the cross-cultural literature we can begin to get a glimpse of the possible root of a man's tendency in our own culture to connect his grief with action.

The least we can expect is to stimulate our own thinking about different ways to express grief. Our own weakness in dealing with grief can be strengthened by observing the strength of the tribal culture's ritual that is so effective in helping their communities come to terms with their loss. With that said, let's look at what can be learned from grief around the world.

Community

One of the first things we notice is the difference between the social structure of indigenous people and our own way of life. Tribal cultures live in communities of intimately interconnected people who are closely affected in some way by the death of any member. They live in close proximity, rely on each other for the necessities of life, and usually have a common history and world view. There is a bond between them that is amplified by the feeling of "us" and "we" that develops when a group of people share such interdependence. The people of these cultures have ritual structures in place that are designed to support those in grief. There is usually a strong expectation and a sense of responsibility that the community will lend its support to those in pain. There is a sense that each death is a loss of the community, not a loss that is isolated.

We can contrast this with our own situation, where there is a certain invisibility in our interdependence. We live together in neighborhoods but not necessarily communities. Many times the neighbors who live three doors down the street have little attachment to or connection with our family. We shop in different places and work in different settings. When a member of a tribe dies, it is a person who was connected in many ways to the community. When a member of a neighborhood in North America dies, too often it is merely someone who lived down the street.

The interdependence of the tribal cultures can be better compared in some ways to the family unit in the United States. Families are interdependent in a similar kind of way, with each member having prescribed roles and duties and interacting on a daily basis. In many ways our families have become our communities. But without the embrace of a larger community we are left with fewer places to receive support for our grief. Our primary means of support frequently is limited to the members of our family. A table with many legs is not affected by one leg being sawed off, but a table with three or four legs is crippled by a similar loss. This is one of the reasons for the emergence of grief counseling in our culture.

World View

Another difference we notice is that the world view of the indigenous people in some way brings meaning to grief. Many times grief is seen as food for the soul of the dead person. The Minianka tribe in Africa see the tears of grief as being nourishment to the newborn soul of the person being grieved. Without the tears the soul could not move beyond the land of the living. In this way the mourners see their grief as a benefit to the person who has died. The variations of this theme are many, but they all incorporate the idea that grief is a necessary process and without it there is some sort of trouble. It is easy to see the contrast to our own culture where people tend to feel that their grief has no purpose or meaning, or worse yet, that it is a selfish act.

Marking the Griever

There are many common themes in the grief rituals among indigenous people. One of these is the tendency to mark the griever. All sorts of mechanisms are used, but one that is found in many cultures is hair. For many tribal people hair is a symbol of life. It marks the passage of time and is therefore connected with life and death. Many times the grievers either cut off their hair or allow their hair and (in the case of the men) beard to grow in response to a death. This is done as a symbolic act and as a part of a ritual process prescribed by the community, but it also functions as a way to mark the mourners. All the people of the community are aware that a certain haircut means a person is grieving. There are many variations on this theme, including special cuts where only a part of the hair is cut or all hair is sheared. The hair can be cut with all sorts of instruments, such as sharpened seashells, or it may be burned off. Sometimes the cut hair is saved as a memorial, to become part of a necklace or be used in a ritual. The important message of the special hair cut is that this is a person in pain, a person who is grieving, and the treatment he receives is altered due to his status as a griever.

Other ways of marking the griever include covering oneself with ashes or oil or certain colors of paint. In one African tribe there is a complex system of designating the colors of grief paint to alert the community to the type of loss that has been suffered. For instance, a man whose father died would wear a certain color of paint in a certain place on the body. If it had been his mother who died, the paint would have been a different color and painted in a different design. This simple system not only alerts the community to the fact that this man is grieving, it also clearly marks the type of loss that has occurred.

Bark

Bark is used in some cultures both as a way to mark the griever and as a symbol of grief. The Karanga people of Africa wear bark to mark themselves as grieving. Women wear a bark necklace, and men wear a woven bark chain around the head. The bark serves also as a symbol of loss, indicating that an individual has been stripped away from the community as bark has been stripped from the tree.

The story of Jaque, also related in a previous chapter, is another example of bark used as a symbol of loss. When his brother died suddenly, Jaque was torn by sadness and anger. Following ancient custom, he went into the forest, selected a tree and, after uttering a prayer, stripped away a piece of the bark. Now the tree, like Jaque, had lost something whose loss caused deep pain. Many times over the following months he returned to visit the tree. As the seasons passed, the wound in the tree healed. So did the wound in Jaque's heart. With the tree as a visible reflection of his loss, Jaque was reminded that he, too, was healing. Jaque is a Native American, a Cree.

In this example, the bark of the tree was used as a symbol of the pain that the man was experiencing. As the bark is a covering of the tree, it is almost as if the man had his own covering sliced away in a similar manner. A part of him was taken—not his core, which still exists—but something that was a part of him all the same. The tree stood as a symbol for his loss; it was wounded in a similar way. Each time he visited that site the tree could remind him of his own wound and, as he watched the tree heal, of his own healing.

These are some of the ways native people have used to mark the griever. Marking gives the griever a public role to play and, in essence, permission to publicly and privately grieve. We can contrast this with the invisibility of grief in our culture. One of the last markings to be discarded in our culture was the black arm band. We now have no overt way to differentiate the people in our community who are grieving from those who are not. The men and women who are grieving can feel this invisibility and the accompanying lack of permission to grieve. Indigenous cultures prescribe specific behaviors and roles for the bereaved, the grief "norm" as it were. This can be contrasted with our own situation where there is confusion over where and when to express grief, or how much grief and of what duration is normal. This lack of "norm" leaves everyone guessing. The people I have worked with have all had the same question, "Is what I'm going through normal?" We are left untethered with a great deal of pain but no box to put it in.

When Does Grief End?

In some tribal communities, it is the responsibility of the community to clearly state when the time of official grief has ended. An example might be that a grieving man was marked by being forbidden to eat a certain type of food. When the community members feel it is the right time, they will offer the particular food to the grieving man as a symbol that he is now ready to re-enter the community as a non-grieving person. There are examples other than food—a certain way of dressing or different behavior—but the essence is the same: the community clearly marks the boundaries of grief for the griever. This contrasts with our own culture where there is great confusion about when and how much grief is appropriate. We live in a near vacuum of social indicators about the time needed to grieve. The most prevalent guideline we have is that many people don't think you should be grieving at all.

Separating Men and Women in Grief

Another form of marking the griever is the separation of men and women in the grief rituals. By separating the grievers these cultures are honoring the differences in grieving between men and women and setting up different containers for healing. An example is the Bara people of southern Madagascar who designate two huts when a death occurs. One hut is the Tranadahy, which means "male house;" the other is the Trano Be Ranomaso, which means the "house of many tears." During the period of time after the death these huts are used for congregating and receiving condolences. The men's hut is the center of activity regarding the death. The men plan and initiate the rituals, receive condolences from the male guests, and take responsibility for the body. The women's hut is more the center of emotional expression, with the women keening, wailing, and crying as they receive condolences from the female guests. These people literally have different places for men and women to be following a death. In this way, men and women are among their own sex and are in a position to be healed by their same-sex community members. It also honors the difference in grieving styles between men and women by allowing the opportunity for each to be near those who grieve as they do.

Ritual

Tribal people have found a box in which to put grief. That box is ritual. The ritual that is used is both a container for the effects of grief and a norm that shows people the way to grieve. It can be any number of activities. For women the ritual many times is related to sharing their pain with each other, crying or keening. Men, on the other hand, usually have a ritual that includes some sort of action—singing sacred songs, drumming, dancing, tree wounding, etc. When Rosenblatt examined grief in 87 different cultures, he did not find a single culture in which men expressed tears more than women. In nine of the cultures studied the men didn't cry at all, and in most of the cases studied the men cried less than the women.[24] This points to a significant difference among men and women: men don't use tears as much as women when dealing with their grief. This finding is not limited to western cultures, as many of the cultures Rosenblatt studied were tribal people who still maintained their grief rituals from their cultural heritage. From this we can see that even in cultures where there is an adequate container for grief the men tend to use tears less often than women. This finding seems to verify the research, regarding a man's decreased levels of prolactin and the increased difficulty for men to access their tears.

What we find when we examine the cross-cultural literature is that men many times have active rituals that help them move into their grief. There is a tribe in Africa where the men literally face the women who are crying and keening in order to get into the mood of grief. They use this activity of watching the women to bring forth their own sense of loss. Even these tribal men with the luxury of intricate and beautiful grief rituals acknowledge that it is not an easy task for them to move into their feeling state. By their actions of facing the women they do something that puts them closer to their own grief.

Drumming

Another active ritual used around the world is that of drumming. The men of the Yoruba in Africa use drumming as an active means to deal with their grief.[25] They have a variety of rhythms for different parts of the funeral service; a rhythm for washing the body, a rhythm for lowering the body into the grave, etc. After the death of a chief the men start playing a specific monotonous grief rhythm over and over. This rhythm is played continuously for three days. The men of the tribe are responsible for keeping the rhythm going and do not allow it to stop. They drum day and night, sleeping in shifts and then drumming for long periods. It is through this ritual, and many others, that the men have something to do after the death, and this activity helps them engage feelings of grief. The rhythm signals to the tribe that a state of mourning exists and is a constant reminder of the loss to the community.

Externalization of Pain

Another aspect of active ritual is the externalization of pain. This is accomplished in a great variety of ways, from lacerating the body, scratching oneself until the blood flows, knocking out a tooth, or even cutting off a finger. Anthropologists tell us the reasons for these mutilations are related to a number of factors encompassed in their world view, including rendering the ghost of the deceased harmless, convincing the soul of the dead of the sincerity of the grief, establishing a corporal union between the living and the dead, strengthening the departed, as an offering, or purification. A few anthropologists have seen the core of these actions: they are outward acts that express inner states. By wounding the body in some way, the inner pain has an outer parallel. This is similar to Jaque who wounded a tree as a symbol; it is just that these people are wounding themselves. As their wounds heal, they will have an outer symbol for the healing of their inner wounds. They will also have physical scars to remind them for some time of the loss that occurred. One Australian tribe has a name for grief that literally translated means "bad guts." That is probably the best description of grief I have ever heard. The mutilations cut away at the "bad guts" and let them flow. There is a ritual among the Aborigines where the blood that is dripping from the mutilated griever is allowed to drip onto the corpse, apparently in an effort to merge the living and the dead and to strengthen the dead person. I am certainly not suggesting that we adopt these rituals as a means to facilitate our own grief. However, they are honest and effective means that these people have found to externalize their pain and "bad guts."

Let's turn now to looking in more detail at the way a particular tribal culture deals with grief. We can examine closely the grief rituals and the mechanisms that the men use in dealing with their grief.

The Yolngu

Our first example is an Aborigine people of Australia, the Yolngu.[26] The men of this tribe begin to work with their grief before a death occurs. As a person becomes seriously ill, the men respond by singing sacred songs. Groups of men gather around the bedside of the ailing person and sing the sacred songs of the tribe. This is not a "let's sing a song and go" routine. The men will sing continuously as the person lies ill. The purpose of the songs is to comfort the dying person, to keep him alert, to insure that the person will die in the right "Manikay" (sacred song cycle), to alert the ancestors that this person is coming to them, and to insure that his soul will be oriented towards its "home" after death. As the men do this, the women of the tribe are responsible for the care of the sick person and feeding the men who are singing. If there is consensus that the person is dying, the women will also cry or keen along with the songs. This crying or keening by the women is called "ngathi." Both the crying and keening and the songs by the men are accompanied by traditional Aborigine instruments, the clapsticks and the didgeridoo. Sometimes the ailing person recovers, and if this happens the singers disperse and life goes on. If death occurs, quiet covers the camp, uncharacteristic of the usual hustle and bustle.

At the ritual announcement of the death, which is made by a man, the women of the tribe keen and wail and throw themselves to the ground. At times they will strike themselves with sharp objects. It is expected that the men of the community will restrain the women from seriously injuring themselves. The men step forward and pull the weapons from the women's hands and throw them out of reach. The women usually respond to this by ceasing their attempts at self-injury. This action of protecting the women is seen as a sign of protection for the grievers, and a show of community support for those who are most affected by the death. It is an action that men can take that is both protecting their loved ones and an indication of their own grief.

The men of the tribe will also keen at times, particularly if the dead person was a close relative, but the more common emotional expression of the men is venting anger by dancing. It is said that the men will dance in an "energetic and violent" manner that signifies hostility. According to Rosenblatt, this expression of hostility directed outward is a common masculine activity following a death. Many times a man's anger will open the door into his other feelings of grief.[27]

Tribal Ritual in the 20th Century

The Yolngu people are in many ways between two worlds. Although they have maintained many of their rituals, they also live in the midst of twentieth century technology. If a member of their tribe has died in the nearby hospital, the body is retrieved in ritual fashion. The community goes to the hospital and obtains the body, then forms a "slow, emotional, and ritualized" procession back to their camp. The body, moved with accompanying dancing and singing, is taken to a shelter where it will lie until burial. It is said that even the cars take part in the ritual, slowing, stopping, starting, and reversing as they mimic the movements of the dancers.

The coffin of the dead person is painted with sacred symbols by the initiated men of the Yolngu. These symbols are secret and are not allowed to be viewed by women and children. The purpose of the sacred symbols is to mediate between the soul of the dead person and the ancestors who will help this newly born soul along his way. Prior to the use of coffins, the Yolngu men would paint the body of the deceased with red ochre and then paint on the sacred symbols.

Singing the Grief

Throughout the days of the ceremonies grief is openly expressed, many times through song. These songs communicate many things: a wish for the return of the dead person, memories of the events in the life of the one who died, and the hope of a safe passageway for the soul to the ancestors. The men often will be singing day and night, and will sleep in shifts as the songs continue. The singing of songs by the men is an important part of the funeral service. They are accompanied by the dancing of the women who enact the stories that the songs are depicting.

The grief that is felt and expressed at the funeral ceremonies can continue for some time. It is said that late at night after the day is done and the tasks of the community are completed, you can sometimes hear the keening of a solitary mourner. The sound is heard throughout the quiet of the community and is accepted as a reminder of the pain and grief that the mourner still feels.

The men are responsible for the ritual activities of their community, and in many ways become like stage managers or directors, making the ritual preparations, rehearsing the songs, and making sure the process runs smoothly. The Yolngu men are active in working with their grief, with very specific activities assigned to them. These activities of singing, dancing, and directing the rituals give the men a framework in which their feelings can emerge and be honored and acknowledged. The women are also busy in keening, crying, dancing, caring for the children, and feeding the men. The men and women of this tribe have very specific roles to play, and both support each other through the difficult period of grief.

The Dagura People

We now turn to another example of indigenous grief rituals, that of the Dagura people of Africa.[28] When a death occurs the women of the village begin to grieve. Their grief is somewhat muted, however, until the men have ritually announced the death. This announcement cannot occur until the men have created a "sacred space" for the grief of the village to emerge, and no man is allowed to show signs of grief until after this ritual space has been created. This is done by invoking the aid of the spirits through a private ritual performed only by the men. The invoking of the spirits is partly designed to elicit enough grief from the mourners to allow the dead person to move into the world of the ancestors. The Dagura believe that the soul's journey into the next world is dependent in some ways upon the grief expressed by the mourners. Without adequate grief, the soul is thought to be stuck on this plane of existence and unable to leave the world. They have thus connected their grief with a purpose, that being the birth of the soul of the newly dead. The creation of ritual space, a safe container for the expression of grief, is seen as essential to the birthing of the spirit of the person who died. A part of this creation of sacred space involves throwing ashes around the house of the deceased and the ritual preparation of an actual physical space for the grief ritual. The announcement states that there has been a death, the ritual space is ready, and it is now time to grieve.

The Dagura Grief Ritual

The grief ritual itself is complex and beautiful. The grieving space is divided into different sections. The body of the dead person is dressed ceremonially and seated on a stool in the section called the "shrine." Two women elders are seated next to the body and are charged with the duty to collect the grief that is being expressed and to "load it on" to the dead person to help him or her in the journey toward the ancestors. The shrine is colorfully decorated and contains some of the important possessions of the dead person. There is a boundary around the shrine which symbolically marks the separation between the living and the dead, and outside of the two women tending to the body, no one is allowed to enter the shrine, for to do so would mean entering the realm of the dead.

Between the shrine and the mourners is an empty space that represents chaos. Within this space people are allowed to express any form of grief they want, as long as it is related to their feelings about the death. Crying, dancing, or any expression of emotion is accepted and expected to take place within this space. There are people who are designated as "containers." These people are often relatives who have come from afar. Their job is to insure the safety of the space for the grievers, making sure that no harm comes to those who are actively grieving. The Dagura believe in releasing grief with all its intensity, but they have also developed a system in which the intensity does not exceed the capacity of the mourners. It is like a system of checks and balances. The containers follow the grievers as they mourn and if they stray out of the ritual space, will gently tap them on the shoulder to remind them to come back into the contained space.

On one side of the shrine are the men of the village and on the other side are the women. Each group consists of mourners and containers. The mourners are further divided by the "kotuosob," a small piece of rope tied around the wrist of the griever. The rope designates a person who was particularly close to the deceased, perhaps a family member. This marking alerts all the participants that someone who is wearing the "kotuosob" is what they call a "center of the heat" person, that is, a person who is more likely to be in danger of "grieving himself to death." The Dagura see grief as food for the psyche, necessary to maintain a healthy psychological balance. But they also see its danger—too much grief and a person will "lose their center" and, they believe, can grieve to death. Thus the Dagura designate specific containers to follow closely behind the tagged person and do exactly as they do, including dancing, jumping to the beat of the drum, or pounding the ground. Sometimes when a tagged griever is experiencing a great deal of grief, a group of containers and mourners will form a line behind him or her with each person in the line doing the same action as the primary griever. It is understood that this transmits the feeling of the primary griever into all of those down the line. This type of process is viewed as a form of silent and physical support to the person who is grieving. It is important to point out that among the Dagura the healing of grief is gender specific. That is, no woman will approach a man in trying to help him with his grief, and no man would do the same for a woman. They believe that it takes a man to help release and heal the grief of another man, and a woman to reflect the grief of a woman.

Music

Music plays an integral part of the ritual. The ceremony is accompanied by xylophones and drums and two singers. The xylophones are divided into male and female. The male xylophone follows the mood of the singers and the female xylophone accompanies the male xylophone with a redundant set of notes. The singers are charged with the responsibility of singing (chanting) the life of the dead person. They sing the joy and sorrow of the family history and the events which led up to the death. This spontaneous singing is done in order to emphasize and direct the grief of the community.

Everyone in the community is expected to take part in this ritual. It is held as a solemn responsibility. Anyone who happens to be near the village during the ritual is expected to participate. It is as if death stops life for a while, all other activities coming to a halt. In the words of one singer, "We are trapped in a world in which we are not in control because of the mighty power of death."

In the Yolngu and Dagura cultures, and in others around the world, grief is vented at the funeral in a very intensive fashion. The rituals of both last about three full days. During that time grief is given all the attention of the community, and it flows and flows. It should also be noted that in both cultures the support for a person's grief does not stop after the funeral. Most indigenous people have post-funeral rituals that provide further opportunity to express grief. Rituals are practiced throughout the year, often marking important dates such as the one-year anniversary of the death. The community expects the grief to continue for some time, and in both the Yolngu and Dagura cultures grief can be released after the funeral and at the next funeral, if need be. This can be compared with our own culture where there is usually very little expression of grief during the funeral services, and few, if any, culturally-endorsed occasions for expressing grief thereafter.

Both the Yolngu and Dagura examples begin to give us an idea of how our culture lacks sufficient contained space to process the emotions that follow a death. Both have woven grief into the fabric of their lives and into their world view. Both cultures have linked a person's grief with the purpose of aiding the soul in its journey. These cultures are very explicit in providing markers of who are the grievers and actions and roles to be played. We have very little of this. Both give men specific things to do following a death, activities that help them in connecting to their grief. Among the Yolngu, men have the responsibility of singing, and with the Dagura, men are responsible for the ritual and the healing of other men.

Imagine just for a moment that the people of the Dagura and the Yolngu suddenly lost their active grief rituals. What would happen to their men and women? What would the men of the Yolngu do without their songs? In some ways this is a parallel of what is happening in our culture. We have much to learn from indigenous people about the resolution of grief. We can use this knowledge to find creative mechanisms that are right for us.

The Basics

We are on dangerous ground when we work with the topic of gender and grief. One of the dangers is that we will lump all men into one pile and all women into another. This is obviously not helpful nor is it accurate. The fact is that we are all unique in our chosen path toward healing, and finding our individual process is a sign of maturity. There are probably more similarities in the way we process grief than there are differences, but there are some significant differences.

The way I have found most useful to understand this is to look at each person's masculine and feminine qualities. We all have both masculine and feminine within; it is our unique balance that makes each of us different. Usually (and I emphasize the usually), men have more of the masculine side and less of the feminine, while for women it tends to be the opposite. But most of us also use both sides of our nature. Women use masculine modes of healing just as men use the feminine. The important thing is finding our unique balance of masculine and feminine energies and honoring our own path.

Below are some basic guidelines about the strengths and needs of the masculine and feminine sides of healing.

What aids the masculine?

- a map of the terrain
- knowing his strength
- linking that strength to action
- linking his action to his pain
- the courage to stand in his tension
- using the future

What aids the feminine?

- a community of support
- verbally sharing her pain
- expressing her pain openly
- completing the past
- relieving her pain through her intimacy with others

Epilogue

Making a Box:
My Father's Death

I was stopped at a red light in my old hometown, only a mile or so from the goal of my brother's house. We were planning to drive together to North Carolina to be with my father who was critically ill. As I waited impatiently at the stoplight, I noticed Sharper's Florist over to the left. It was the same place I had stood as a young man nervously picking out a corsage for my date—floods of memories went through my mind as the light no longer seemed a nuisance but a blessing. I noticed the liquor store straight ahead where my father and I had been many times before, picking out the beer of the week. We both liked German beer.

The light finally turned green. I made a left turn and drove through the poor section of our hometown, remembering how each Thanksgiving my family would be together. I also remembered how my father would take some time out of each Thanksgiving Day to make sure there was no one hungry in the surrounding neighborhoods. I can remember as a young boy going with him to deliver food. I was scared; I had never been into this part of town this deeply before. My father seemed unaware of any danger and went calmly about his business. The people we went to seemed to know him and gratefully accepted what he offered. My father seemed able to give away the food in a way that honored the recipient, in a way that turned what could have been an arrogant act into an act of humility on his part. He would stop at each place and talk a little, which I remember totally pissed me off. I wanted to get the hell out of there, but my father wanted to be sure everyone had food. If he found someone who didn't have food, he would take the time to go back and get more. That's the kind of man he was.

I pulled into the bluestone circular driveway of my brother's house, the same driveway I had driven into so many times before. This had once been my childhood home, then my wife and I bought it from my folks and later sold it to my brother Joel. The crunch of the bluestones as they passed beneath my tires brought back more memories. I got out of the car and Joel was there to meet me. We hugged and Joel said Dad had "passed away" just an hour ago. I was in shock. The first thought that hit me was "Hey Joel, why are you using euphemisms?" but I said nothing of this to him. It brought back a memory of working at a counseling center for death and dying in Washington, D.C. Father William Wendt, the director, was a powerful man whose deep, rumbling voice I imagined to be surpassed only by God's. One day a new counselor was introducing herself in our monthly staff meeting. Talking a bit about her own grief history, she said, "We lost my mother last summer." From the back of the small room came Father Wendt's unmistakable voice, "Where'd you lose her?" The new counselor looked like she wanted to melt down into the couch. Bill had made a point in a way only he could do: people don't pass away; people die.

I was lost for a while, though. I went through the motions of talking with my brother's family, discussing when we should leave. I could hear myself talking, but it seemed as though someone else was speaking instead of me. There was a distance between my actions and my brain, as if I were in someone else's movie. Then I decided to call my mother. We talked for a short while and I told her that I wanted to speak at my father's memorial service. She told me that I didn't have to, that it might be difficult. And then it happened—the tears started to flow out of my gut amidst strange, almost animal-like noises. It began when I said to my mother that I wanted other people to know what it was like to grow up with a great man like my father, and only one of us could do that These words took about a millennium to come out, interspersed with tears like a syncopated ratchet in the hands of a two-year-old. Although it sounded bad, it felt good. My father had been ill for about six months and during that time I had experienced a great deal of sadness but no tears. Now they were flowing.

I did speak at my father's memorial service, and it was an important and powerful experience. Through the action of speaking and preparing for the service, I found a container for bits and pieces of my grief. The word "container" is meant to describe anything that allows us to move from an ordinary state of awareness into the experience of pain, and then lets us move out of the pain again. Women often will use verbal and emotional interaction as a means of containing their pain, while men often will prefer an active container.

Only in retrospect have I realized how ironic it seems that one of the active containers I found for my grief that week was actually building a container. Joel and I decided to design and make the container for my father's ashes. During the week of the funeral we spent a lot of time in the garage, which had doubled as my father's workshop, planning and constructing this memorial container. As we worked, my brother and I would share stories about my father. We used his tools and his wood. One of the most important aspects for us was the presence of my father's eighty-year-old best friend, Charlie Beamen. Charlie was a retired minister who had been my father's woodworking buddy. As the three of us worked together we exchanged numerous tales of my father. Joel and I told Charlie of our experiences growing up with Dad, and Charlie told us of his exploits with my father in the recent past. As we worked and told stories, the tears and laughter flowed.

We men had found a safe place to act as a "container" for our emotions. The workshop functioned in this manner to connect our pain and tears with a project. The project became a "hook" for our pain. That week, the men who came to visit our family tended to be drawn to the workshop. They usually had ideas or comments about the work that was being done, and gladly chipped in to aid in making the container.

The women visitors, however, were more likely to spend time inside talking. These boundaries were not solid; we men spent plenty of time in the house talking with visitors about my father and what he meant to us, and the women would sometimes boldly venture into the workshop area. It was not that the men and women were separated, but that the men and women each had specific tasks that were many times intermingled.

 One of the reasons that men tend to have an easier time in connecting their grief with action is that men have a harder time in connecting their emotions with words. Women have greater skill in this arena, and are usually more drawn to connecting their pain, tears, and grief on a verbal level to their most intimate friends and family. It needs to be said that each person's grief is unique to them, and by separating men and women we are in dangerous territory. There are general differences in the way men and women grieve but there are probably more individual differences.

This preference for action puts men in a precarious state when grief strikes because in our culture almost all of the activities related to death have been contracted out. Activities such as building the coffin, directing the ritual, giving the eulogy, digging the grave, and the funeral itself have been turned over to the "death professionals." This leaves men with nothing to do following a death, negating many men's strength of action. It is a difficult task for men to stand in a funeral home with nothing to do.

Without any sanctioned grief rituals men have had to be creative in finding workable containers. Abraham Lincoln had a male friend who would come to the White House at his request and sing what Lincoln called "sad songs." This man and Lincoln would walk quietly to a certain room in the White House where the man would proceed to sing. During these activities Lincoln would sit quietly and cry. Was Lincoln dealing with his grief? Undoubtedly. Did those around Lincoln know of this activity? Probably not. Many times the activity a man chooses (often this is not a conscious decision, but done instinctively) to contain his grief is not highly visible to those around him. This invisibility leads many to believe that the man is not grieving. This is simply not so.

There are many containers that men use to deal with the chaos of their grief. Writing functions for me as a container for my grief. Through the act of writing I come into contact with my pain. Interestingly, the writing takes on a more powerful capacity when I read aloud to others what I have written about my grief. It is somehow more natural to read what I have written (usually through my tears) than to sit and talk about my feelings. Writing now about my father's death and the containers I found to deal with my pain has provided me with yet another container where I can listen in safety to the echoes of my grief.

Singing the Grief:
My Eulogy for My Father

The funeral service was the next morning. I had been thinking all week—what could I say about my father that would encapsulate my respect and love for him? The task was overwhelming; there were no words big enough. My mother had requested that I speak for only five minutes or so in order to keep the length of the service from being burdensome. It seemed impossible to imagine what I could say in five minutes that would do what I wanted. I made a few notes that week, but mostly relied on Spirit to tell me what the hell to do.

The next day as our family walked into the church, I could feel the closeness of my emotions. We sat down in the pew and, as it turned out, my father's brother, Uncle Jake, and my six-year-old son Luke were sitting on either side of me. Both were blessings. The organist started playing a Barber piece adapted for organ, "Adagio for

Strings." The first few bars were enough to ignite all the emotion that was in me. Once I realized what was being played, I blurted out a loud "Oh no!" That piece was a favorite of my father's and mine. He had introduced me to Barber's music and to the choral arrangement of this piece in particular. I knew it was a piece that he wanted played at his funeral. Earlier in the summer we had spoken of this service and his desires about the music and other arrangements. To hear that piece now was too much. I went into a crying spell, with Uncle Jake on one side feeding me tissues (which I hadn't even thought to bring), and Luke on my other side, his little arms wrapped around my leg and knee, giving me loving pats. Luke said nothing, but his patting my leg said loudly and clearly, "It's OK, Dad."

I was confused: here was the son taking care of the father. At first I felt a little guilty, thinking "He shouldn't have to do that." But I didn't have any choice. I began to have real doubts about whether I would be able to speak. I decided that if I couldn't speak—just got up there and blubbered tears—that was a testimony in itself, and so be it.

I realized as I sat there that I was between the two generations, my father's generation on my left and my son's on my right. I had a strong sense of the cycle of life and death, its wheel-like nature, and my position on the wheel.

The more the music played the more the tears came. I was really beginning to wonder whether I would speak or blubber. When it came time for me to get up, I looked toward Uncle Jake and he kind of nodded. I had decided to attempt to put myself into neutral and allow "whatever" to speak through me. It really wasn't much of a decision because I didn't have any other choice. The following is the text of what was spoken through me:

"I have been having a lot of feelings since my father's illness and death and we will see how long the feelings will allow me to speak.

By far the biggest feeling I have had has been gratefulness. Gratefulness to have stood in the shade of my father's tree. Because to me, my father was like a tree in many ways. An oak tree. An oak who's taproot was anchored in faith and in the Divine, and with branches and leaves that act as a home for those around. I stood in that home and for that I am so grateful. It's an experience that I wish I could condense into a couple of words and then tell you.

My father's tree was stable, you couldn't push it, it was strong. It was a place for everyone around him to glow. He wanted others to glow. He enjoyed and reveled in the glow of everyone around him...not only his own. It is a beautiful thing for a man to be able to do that. I honor him for that. And boy, do I feel a little dwarfed by comparison. A couple of weeks ago I told him, 'Dad, you have always done things so deliberately and calmly. You have been a great role model for me. I just feel so overwhelmed by trying to follow in your footsteps.' He looked at me and motioned with his hand as if throwing a ball at me and said, 'Oh, you're all right.' Somehow that 'oh, you're all right' was the biggest blessing. He had told me many times that he loved me, that he was proud of what I did, but this sunk deeply into me, and I felt it as a blessing from him like I had never received before. All the times my father told me of his love for me or how he was proud of what I was doing were still with me, but this simple phrase moved me in a unique way.

I think I can speak for all of my siblings when I say that we always knew within our family that we were loved. It was not just we Goldens, however. Young people would come up to my father to be listened to, to be heard and understood. Both my mother and father had the capacity to be with someone and to hear them without judgment. Maybe a little judgment, but not much. That's a rare commodity that you don't see very much. I was blessed to be there.

I see my father's tree as being linked with passion. Probably not the passion you think I'm talking about. I'm talking about a passion that takes an everyday moment and turns it into something joyful. Now I could give you 15 examples of this, but one was our dinner table at home. When we had dinner we didn't just have dinner. My father and mother would devise things to do at the dinner table. Sometimes it was that you couldn't say anything without rhyming. So whatever was said at the table had to rhyme, like 'Peas, please' or 'I know I shouldn't oudda but please pass the budda.' We had fun. My father was able to put joy into everyday moments.

My father was also a wise man, an intelligent man. I remember last summer I told my father that I had taken every bit of advice he had ever given me, it had just taken 10 to 20 years to implement it. He and I both laughed when I said this. But there is something in this story, and that something is that he allowed me to fumble the ball, to make mistakes, and to screw up. He would make his opinions known, but he let me go my own way and make my own mistakes. I knew his love for me even if I didn't follow what he wanted for me. To me, that is loving wisdom.

My father was also a man of action. Not only did he have it up here (pointing to head), he had it in his feet too. Thanksgiving at my house was always a time for the family to be together, but I always will remember that my father would give up a bit of that day to make sure that the people who lived near us had food. I honor his action.

My father was also a man who knew how to build bridges, to connect things and to bless things. When I was in my father's presence, I felt his blessing and a connection to him.

There is one last reason the oak tree is a good symbol for my father: acorns. My mother's yard now is covered in acorns. You can't take a step without smushing a handful into the ground. To me these acorns are a sign of my father and all of his blessings I have spoken of, plus a lot more. All of his blessings are left as seeds which can sprout now on their own. When I see an acorn now I'll think of my father, remember his blessings, and try to pass on the seed to others."

Eulogies are one of the last remnants of active grief rituals in our culture. During the Potlatch ceremony of the native peoples of northwest North America, men sing "sorry songs" that chronicle the life of the deceased. These are not memorized songs, but spontaneous expressions of grief through "singing" the life of the person who died. The Dagura men of Africa dance out their grief, and the Ylongu men of Australia sing and dance their grief. The men of these various cultures are familiar with these activities and their use; they have seen other men in their communities perform these rituals for as long as they can remember. The rituals are a part of their realities, and when the time comes, they have a "friendly tool" to use in dealing with their grief. Giving a eulogy is similar to "singing the life" of the person who died. We can chronicle the events of the person's life and state how that person impacted our being. By making a public statement we honor the life of the person.

It was my experience, and that of other men I have known who have given eulogies, that it was an important event in our lives. The memory of speaking, or sometimes writing, carries on through the cycle of grief and becomes a marker for the experience. By remembering the act of speaking, we connect with the feelings that were present at the time and those that continue. Somehow it is easier to remember the act of speaking and the associated feelings than to simply "remember" how one felt. It is easier to talk about the eulogy you gave than simply talking about the feelings. The act becomes a hook for the expression of emotion, even as the grief continues.

Fixing a Hole:
Grieving With Other Men

There I was dripping in sweat, the kind that rolls down the side of your head and innocently into your ear. The still summer evening was allowing me to hear my own breath and my own thoughts. I was determined to make this a great hole and I kept digging—probably farther than I really needed to, but on I went. What seemed like a great deal of sweat was swallowed effortlessly by the hole, absorbed as a matter of course by the dirt in the bottom. The hole and the dirt were equally unmoved by the tears I shed.

This hole was to be the home of a tree that was being given as a memorial to my father who had died the previous November. I had known the hole needed digging, but had put off the task until now—now being just about the last possible moment it could be dug. As I continued digging, I found myself flooded with memories of my father. My thoughts moved back and forth between recent events leading up to his death and childhood experiences. I remembered his engineering talents and nature and tried to dig the hole in a way that would please him.

As I dug, the feelings flowed through me: the sadness of missing him, the gratefulness of having been his son, and the anger and frustration of my powerlessness. All of these feelings found their way into this hole. The act of digging became an avenue for the various thoughts and feelings to arise. Through the action I was opened to my own inner world.

I started wondering why I had put off this job, then realized that I hadn't, and didn't, want to do it. Actually digging the hole brought the death more into reality, and a part of me didn't want that. I've learned to accept this part of me that wants to deny things. Denial is not really such a bad thing, and it doesn't go away as quickly as some people seem to think. I've noticed it has a slow, zigzag decay that can last a long time. In a way, denial can be our friend, allowing us to slowly accept the reality at hand. I became aware of the battle going on between the denying part and the digging-the-hole part. As a friend of mine says, "We have wetware, not hardware."

The tree was planted in an emotional ritual attended by myself and the six men who donated the tree. The activity became an avenue for all of us to delve into our interiors and connect with a variety of issues, from relationships with our fathers to the finality of death. The activity of buying, digging, planting, and gathering together became a hub for a wide variety of spin-offs. As we stood around the tree, we all had a chance to speak and to listen, and somehow having an activity made this process flow smoothly. It would have been much more difficult to simply sit in a circle and talk about our feelings. It was through the doing that we could connect.

Death professionals have long been confounded by the difference in men and women in visiting gravesites, which is that the men tend to visit more often. My own experiences have given me a deeper understanding of why this takes place. Men tend toward linking their grief with a place, action, or thing. There have been many examples presented in this book: the man who wore his deceased daughter's ring as a remembrance of her, the man who carved a bust of his wife after her death, the man who built a pond in memory of his murdered brother, the man who wore his father's watch, and so on. These activities are often quiet and unseen by most people. The casual observer might assume that the man is "not grieving," but that is many times not the case.

I have found a wide variety of activities that, like planting the tree, help me in connecting to my inner spheres. Writing, gardening, and music are examples. All of these activities can take me into myself and my grief and joy.

Another activity I have used is a ritual practiced by Cree Indians, as discussed in chapter seven. Tree wounding is a simple and beautiful ritual. Following ancient custom, Cree men who are grieving go into the forest, select a tree, and after uttering a prayer, strip away a piece of the bark. Now the tree, like the man, has lost something whose loss causes deep pain. Many times over the following months the man will return to visit the tree. As the seasons pass, the wound in the tree heals, and so does the wound in the man's heart. With the tree as a visible reflection of his loss, the man is reminded that he, too, is healing.

In this ritual there is both an action and a place, and both serve as "containers" or "hooks" for the inner state of the man. As the man performs the action or visits the place, he is afforded the opportunity to experience his pain and to have his healing reflected back to him. I have used this ritual a number of times and have found it extremely helpful. The trees I have chosen are mostly in my back yard, and they stand as reminders to me of my grief, pain, and healing.

The use of activity as a means to connect with one's grief is not exclusive to men; women also find this approach helpful. The difference is that women have a strength in connecting their emotions to their words and then are inclined to "share" those words with the people in their life whom they love. This proclivity fits nicely with the keyword of "intimacy" that Deborah Tannen used to describe women in her book *You Just Don't Understand*. According to Tannen, a woman's world revolves around her intimacy and connection with others. We would expect that when a woman experiences the chaos of grief, a primary mode of healing will be connecting her pain with her intimacy to others.

Tannen uses the keyword of "independence" for men. When independence is your keyword, you are probably less likely to want to "share" your feelings with those around you. You will be more likely to seek out modes of healing that will be harmonious with your interest in maintaining independence. I know for myself, and for many men, the verbal connection is facilitated by linking it with some action, place, or thing. I am less inclined to simply "share" my feelings with those around me. I am grieving, but I do it in my own way, a way that is more quiet and less visible and harmonizes with my interest in independence. It is for this reason that it is unwise to judge a man's grief by how much he "shares" it with others. A man's pain cannot be judged by outer appearances or the abundance of tears. All people are unique in the ways they find to heal themselves. There are probably more individual differences in grief than there are gender differences, but the gender differences do exist and need to be honored.

My father's memorial tree now stands in a park that is adjacent to my home. Not only was the activity surrounding the tree helpful, now the tree has moved from being an activity to being a place. Each time I come or go I see that tree sitting there, being itself. When I see the tree I am reminded of my father, my grief, and the men who lovingly honored both my father and my pain.

Playing Catch:
Stewarding Children's Grief

My son and I were playing a friendly game of catch. As I tossed him the ball, I noticed the mitt he was wearing. It had been my father's baseball glove which he had used when I was in Little League. I remembered the many times my father had gone to Little League practice and coached or hit fly balls to us. Sports were not really his forte, but being part of my life was important to him. A scientist and researcher with NASA, he was a dedicated father who enjoyed spending time with his three children and involving himself with their separate interests.

My seven-year-old son Luke had chosen that particular glove as his own, perhaps because it was old and very flexible and perhaps due to its having been his grandfather's. This glove has given us many opportunities to talk about my father and his death. As we toss the ball back and forth, it is a link into my father and his history. Luke and I have had many of these conversations, usually quick and to the point. Luke might make a particularly good catch and then say it was the glove that helped him with such a spectacular play. I then might say, "Yeah, that's a special glove. I sure do miss Granddaddy." Luke agrees and points out that he misses his sense of humor; the game goes on. These short interludes serve us both as a way to remember and honor our pain at the loss of my father and his grandfather. Healing grief is a matter of chipping away at the potent feelings over and over again. Taking small chunks during an activity such as playing catch is certainly a valid form of healing.

My daughter Julia, who is 13 years old, has a very different way to approach her pain. Julia will approach me and request "special time," meaning we are to sit and talk about something. She says, "I miss Granddaddy," and proceeds to talk of her feelings of loss. She already has the agenda and will happily orchestrate the conversation. This too is a valid form of healing.

A part of the reason for the difference between Julia and Luke is their age. Julia is more developed physically/psychologically and has a more sophisticated understanding of her emotions. But there is also a difference that has to do with gender. Luke loves to do things and maybe talk some while we are actively participating together. I learn more about Luke and his life while we are wrestling than any other time. We will be grunting and groaning as we push at each other's body, and all of the sudden he will stop and say something about his day. Just as quickly we are back at it again. This pattern continues, with brief flashes of self-disclosure during activities.

Julia, however, doesn't seem to need the activity. She needs the emotional contact and attention. Both ways are healing, both need to be honored. Although I believe this is a gender difference, it could easily go the other way, with my daughter preferring activity and my son more inclined to talk. It is not that boys do it one way and girls another. It is that as parents we are responsible for finding our children's individual gifts in healing themselves and then helping them use it. Grief is a potent force, and we need to find ways to steward our children's connection with feelings of loss and their healing.

Grief is no different than any other process that children learn. As parents we steward our children's anger, homework, sexuality, social skills, bathroom behavior, and a long list of many others. We tend to be more active in our assistance with the younger ones and expect more from children as they grow and mature. We make decisions about what the child needs to know at any given time and find ways to teach them the next level when they are ready. Homework might be a good example. Think of a very young child and how you help them with their studies. Usually we tend to be more active in finding an appropriate place for them to work and are also active in our help with their learning. As the child grows older, we expect and teach different things. We do less of the actual work and more teaching of skills in how to work. This is stewardship. We give to them what they need at any given time, based on our understanding of their individual qualities and their level of development.

Stewarding a child's grief is the same. We adjust our approach to their pain based on their level of development and our assessment of their needs. But stewarding grief is a tough task for parents who are actively grieving themselves. It is often a time when our "parent" energy to teach, help, and engage our kids is at an all time low. We too are in need of healing. The saving grace, however, is that by stewarding our children's grief we ourselves heal. Each time I have a burst of a conversation with Luke about my father, or each time Julia asks me for "special time," I get in touch with my grief and loss related to my father's death. By stewarding I am also healing.

Sometimes parents want to hide their feelings of grief and loss from their kids. Occasionally this can be appropriate, but usually if the parent holds back it stops the healing for both parent and child. The kids sense that there is something not being said and will pick up that this "holding back" must be the adult way to do things. We need to be open with our kids about our grief in a way that helps them to see that we are grieving. When we allow our kids to see our grief we give them the best teaching we could give: a role model. This can be helpful to both parents and children.

Families can heal together in a number of ways. One of the most basic ways is to make sure that the name of the person who died is spoken in your household.Speaking the name of the person has a powerful effect. If the name is not spoken, it sets up a situation where it seems that the topic of this person (or pet?) is not one that is open for conversation. Saying the name out loud states clearly that the topic is indeed open. Children will respond to this in their own way. Watch carefully how they respond and you will learn their ways of healing.

Speaking the name can manifest in a number of ways; it does not have to be on a rigid schedule or formally spoken. The best ways I have found are to bring up my father's name in spontaneous situations. For example, as we are having dinner I might mention my father's love of something related to what we are talking about. This gives a green light for the kids (or the adults) to speak up if they wish, or to remain silent—both are acceptable. Sometimes kids have very introverted ways of healing and can benefit from listening to another's conversation. We need to honor all ways.

Another way of speaking the name is to include the person's name in the prayers you use, such as requesting special blessings for this person or using a prayer that may have been a favorite of his or hers.

A related idea is to have pictures of the person who died in different places in your home. In my house we have pictures of my father on the refrigerator, stuck to some cabinets, and in some other spots. This has a similar effect as speaking the name. It includes and honors the person who died and gives a similar green light for discussion and healing.

Creating family activities in honor of the person who died is a great way to accommodate all of the differences within your family. The activity allows both a place to talk about the loss and an opportunity to connect one's action with the grief. Let's say the person who died loved to fish. In this case you might plan a family activity for everyone to go fishing. You make it clear that this trip is in honor of the person who died. On the trip you make sure that the person's name is spoken and that the participants know the nature of the honoring. If conversations come up about the person, that is great; if not, that is okay too.

Doing something together as a family in honor of the person who died is healing in itself. What generally happens is that the kids get into it in their own ways. I know in my family, Luke would say that he is going to catch the biggest fish for Granddaddy. In that way he connects the trip and his action (fishing) with his grief for his grandfather. There is healing in this. The activity provides a "ground" in which the entire family can plant the seeds of their grief in their own way. Some family members may talk and cry about the loss while others, like Luke, may connect their pain and tears with their goal to catch the biggest fish. This same idea is important with regard to holidays and anniversaries. There are many ways to honor the person who died and you can use your creativity to find an activity that fits your family.

A traditional form of the activity idea is that of visiting the grave, but often this is impractical due to distance or other reasons. The kids also sometimes think it is "dumb." A variation on this is to create a place that becomes linked to the person who died. Maybe that person had a favorite spot, or maybe your family has a beautiful spot that everyone enjoys visiting. As a parent you can link that spot with the person who died. You can declare it a spot that the person who died loved (or would have loved), and your family visits there can include the memories of this person. It might be a waterfall, or like a family I know, an amusement park. No words need be spoken as long as the family knows the link has been made. Most times I think you will find that the person becomes a topic of discussion when visiting that place.

Another family I know created a needlework memorial in honor of a family member who had died. The father laid out the pattern and the mother and children did the cross-stitch sewing. With the help of the kids, the father made a frame, and the needlework was dedicated to the person who died and put in a place of honor in the family home. It was a family project that used everyone's energy and involved everyone in the healing process. The examples could go on and on: one family put together a video, another created a sculpture for their yard. The important point is that these families found a project that could be used as a means of honoring the person who died while at the same time giving the family a joint space to honor their grief. By doing things together as a family in honor of the person who died, you are creating a healing space for the whole family.

As parents we need to find a variety of ways to help ourselves and our family heal our grief and pain. By doing it together we not only heal, we come closer as a family unit. Helping Luke and Julia heal from the loss of their grandfather has helped me heal from the loss of my father, and our shared grief has brought us all closer together.

Decorating the Tree:
A Family Ritual for the Year Anniversary

It has been one year now since my father's death. In some ways it seems like ten years and in other ways it seems like ten minutes. My brother and I went to Greensboro, North Carolina, to spend some time with my mother to honor this anniversary. We worked together to plant a tree in honor of my dad, and it was good to be together in our grief.

After I returned from North Carolina I began wondering how to honor my dad within my own family. I was having some difficulty in coming up with something that felt right. About that time my wife Darbie came up to me and said, "Hey, I have an idea." She suggested that we decorate the tree that had been donated by my male friends and planted in the park adjacent to our home. What a great idea!

We discussed how we could all work together making the decorations and putting them on the tree.

I started by gathering some berries and dried flowers from my garden. As I strung together orange nandina berries, purple beauty-berry bush berries, and some dried up purple and white gomphrena flowers, I was with my father. I felt the sadness of his absence. I experienced the profound gratefulness at having been his son. I thought of what he would have preferred and took those preferences into account in making the decorations. I marveled at how the idea resonated with what I thought he would appreciate—the decorations were natural and would serve not only as decorations but also as food for the wildlife that inhabits our corner of the woods. A perfect way to honor and remember my father.

By the time the kids arrived home from school, Darbie and I had gathered all of the berries, string, pine cones, flowers, carrot pieces, etc., and we all sat together making the decorations. As we did this we talked of my dad and what he meant to us. When we finished (on the actual anniversary of his death), we went out into the rain to adorn the tree and have a short ritual.

Darbie was wise in her suggestion of a family activity, for it is a great example of how people can be of help to men in their grief. Her idea allowed us to plan, discuss, and carry out a family project, and in the process remember my father and our grief for him. Through the "doing" our family had the opportunity to experience the "being" of the grief. As a man, it helped me to connect with my grief through a task that involved our entire family, rather than grieving alone. Everyone in our family had a chance to remember my dad by being involved as a family in an activity that honored him.

What are other ways that people can help men in their grief? Please know that we can't say all men grieve like "this" and all women like "that." Everyone is unique in his or her path toward healing. The following ideas will be generally applicable to men, but could very well be helpful to anyone.

One idea is to avoid asking a man how he feels. Have you ever done this before? What do you get in response? Most times, I bet you get "Oh, I'm doing okay" or "Fine" or something like that. Why does this happen? In *You Just Don't Understand*, Deborah Tannen explains that conversations such as this are tiny rituals. They are not meant for information exchange as much as they are meant to helps us in negotiating our everyday "hellos" and "good-byes." When you ask a man what he is feeling, he will many times respond automatically that he is doing fine. This is a male (and sometimes female) cultural ritual that brings a response that is sometimes not what the questioner had in mind. Perhaps a better question would be "What is the toughest thing about your loss?" This question avoids the mechanical "ritual" response and also honors a man's hierarchical nature. The men I have known have often mentally gauged the most difficult aspects of their loss and have some familiarity with this way of looking at things. The question also overtly honors that grief is a struggle and tacitly honors the man for being engaged in this struggle.

In general, men seem to have a different way of connecting to their grief, and often this way is not related to talking. I can remember a couple who came to see me for therapy where the wife's complaint was that the husband didn't talk about his feelings. The woman was a therapist herself and the man was a construction worker. It was clear that they loved each other dearly, but were having some tough times in talking about things. I noticed that often the wife would ask the husband how he was feeling, he would pause, and after a short period she would proceed to tell him how he was feeling. She was usually right, but she did not give him the opportunity to express his feelings. The next time this happened, I suggested that we give him time to come up with his own answer. Well....we waited and waited for what seemed to be a long time. Five minutes went by, and then almost ten. I was afraid I had really screwed up—had I put him into an impossible situation? Then he finally spoke and proceeded to speak from his heart in a way that astounded his wife. We all learned that he was capable of finding his heart, he just needed more time.

Men seem to have different mental processors for feelings. Maybe a good way to describe it would be to say that it's like having different computers: men have a 286 and women have Pentiums when it comes to processing emotions mentally. There is absolutely nothing wrong with a 286—it's just slower. Give men a chance to express their feelings, give them time.

One way to give men more time is to write to them rather than talk to them. Writing a note gives the man freedom to read it more than once, to take it with him to work or the john, and importantly, to respond in his own time. Another benefit is that writing takes the non-verbal communication and the "tone of voice" out of the equation. I know couples who have a terrible time in talking about their grief, but when they start writing notes to each other they gain a greater understanding. Give it a try.

Another important thing to note about men and grief is the tendency for men to withdraw when they are actively grieving. The purpose of the withdrawal is often not to avoid those close to them or to avoid the grief, but is related to a man's desire to find some inner understanding and balance before moving the pain out into the "open." Men tend to view grief as a burden and a problem, and they are steadfast in their desire to solve their own problem and not "dump" it on someone who has no responsibility for the grief.

This contrasts with the more feminine mode of "sharing" the grief and thereby bringing greater intimacy with her loved ones. For years the grief research showed that men grieve "less" than women. Then we found out why this happens. When drawing research samples for grief studies, the women who would volunteer would usually be in a great deal of pain and in the midst of the chaos of grief. They tended to be interested in "sharing" this pain with the researchers. The men, on the other hand, who were experiencing a similar intensity of grief did all they could to avoid being a part of these studies. The men who would participate were those who had already withdrawn and had found a certain handle on things. Therefore, the results from these studies indicated that women grieved more than men. We know now that this is not so, but is a function of a biased sample.

It is probably good to honor a man's need to withdraw to gain some balance. There are numerous masculine role models for this activity, Christ being one. My own reading of the Bible tells me that when Christ was in need of healing he would withdraw "to the desert." This does not mean that men shouldn't talk about their grief. Talking about grief and connecting with one's emotions in the process is healing for all people. It does mean that men will usually withdraw first and talk later.

Because of a man's tendency to withdraw, his inclination to grieve through activity, and societal shaming of tender emotions, a man's pain tends to be more invisible than a woman's. If you want to connect with a man in his grief, keep in mind that he will often have an easier time connecting to his pain through activity, that he will have a tendency to withdraw initially, and that he will probably be less agile in his verbal processing of his pain. Maybe knowing this will help in finding ways of honoring men in their grief. I think Darbie's willingness to connect with me through planning an activity and ritual for our family has deepened our intimacy while honoring our different paths.

Listening to the Music:
When Grief Recedes

There we were, my seven-year-old son Luke and I, sprawled out on the family room floor building a model rocket he had received as a Christmas gift. I had put a number of CD's in the changer and the one randomly selected was blues man Johnnie Johnston. As Luke and I worked on the rocket, I started to notice the music more and more until I got up and turned the volume up a notch or two. We worked a little more, and both Luke and I were starting to move with the music, so I said to him, "You want it a little louder?" He responded in the affirmative, and when I got up this time I really cranked it. The extra volume was wonderful. As I enjoyed the loud music, something snapped inside me. This was not a muscle pull snap, this was a nonphysical, subtle snap that caught my attention. It felt like it was in my chest, but the "where" wasn't really important. What was important was that the snap had seemingly opened up an old familiar joy, a joy I hadn't felt since my father's illness and death. It was as if a governor had been taken off an engine. My joy was able to run again at what seemed to be full throttle. Now we both forgot about the rocket and just joyfully bounced along with the music. It was the first time in many months that I could remember listening to music with such powerful pleasure.

I had not consciously or intentionally avoided listening to the music I love, but I hadn't listened much since my father's death a year before. I didn't even realize I had avoided it until I felt myself truly enjoying it again. This made me think of other things that I have traditionally done for enjoyment. Drumming came to mind. I have played percussion instruments since I was a young boy. From rock and jazz to orchestral or concert band music to hand drumming, I have loved the percussive instruments. When I started to think about my lack of joyful time spent with my music, I realized that I hadn't played my drums for about the same period. I chuckled at the thought that it appeared that I had been punishing myself. It wasn't a punishment, just that I didn't feel like it. As simple as that.

I had been fairly conscious of the advent and process of my grief as it came to me in various ways over the year since my father's death. What has been interesting to note is that it has seemed to be easier to see it coming than to see it going! I think, in general, grief's arrival is more obvious than its departure. It makes me think about being at the ocean, sitting at the beach, and noticing how the tide is coming in. The rising tide calls to us and grabs our attention as we move out of its way. The receding tide, however, seems to be more subtle and less demanding of our awareness. I think the same is true for grief. When grief enters our system it often comes with a shock—jarring us out of a "comfortable" state.

But its exit is much more subtle and quiet.

Many of us celebrate when grief starts to recede, but there are a number of things that can complicate grief's gradual departure. One of the most difficult aspects I have seen is that some people start to worry that they will somehow forget the person who died. The fear seems to be that without the grief the person will cease to abide in the griever's memory. This brings a difficult state where the grieving person grows increasingly ambivalent about his or her grief. On one hand, they fear that if they stop grieving their loved one will be "forgotten," and on the other hand, they are ready to be done with the grief! Other scenarios include fearing to dishonor the loved one if they stop grieving. The thought seems to be "I haven't grieved enough considering how much I loved him (or her)." The question is "Have I grieved enough?"

This is a tough question in our culture where we lack markers and community involvement with our grief, but we can look to tribal cultures to find some interesting responses to this problem of knowing when someone has "grieved enough." There is a tribe in Africa that takes very seriously the idea of letting people know when their grief is "ripe." This tribe prohibits the grieving person from ingesting a certain food during the time of grief. During the mourning period, the elders of the tribe keep watch over the individual and monitor his or her state of grief and path toward healing. When the elders decide that the person is ready, a ritual is begun. During this ritual the people of the tribe ceremoniously bring to the grieving person a meal containing the previously forbidden food. This acts as a marker for the griever that a phase of the grief has been completed. The community rejoices together in the "return" of the individual to the community. In this way, the community acts as a support and a feedback mechanism to aid the person in dealing with the elusive nature of grief. The community joins in helping to gauge when the individual has "grieved enough." Imagine for a moment that the "elders" of your community had done this for you. What would that be like?

There are other tribes in Africa who paint intricate designs on their bodies to depict the details of the state of their grief. These painted designs alert the community to the type of loss that occurred, how long ago it occurred, and other details of the grief. In this way everything is above board and out in the open for all to see. Imagine what it would be like in our culture if we wore our loss history on our bodies—or maybe on our cars! How would it change your experience to drive in rush hour knowing the loss history of the drivers of the cars around you? Knowing about these tribal customs is interesting and teaches us what we don't have in our culture. It also shows us that, when it comes to healing grief, we are truly the "primitives."

Unlike tribal people, we don't usually live in supportive communities that know of our grief and our healing. Without this, we are in more need of help in our struggle with the elusiveness of grief. Whether it is coming or going, grief can be a very elusive beast. It is so elusive that it often can help us to link our grief with a picture or image that can act as a way to clarify our healing. An image that comes to my mind is to think of grief as being like a cloud. Think for a second of what kind of cloud your grief would look like today? Do you have "clear skies" or is your cloud more fog-like, permeating everything and making it difficult to see even things that are close by. Or it might be more like a torrential thunderstorm, with lightning, strong damaging wind, and rain so thick that you can't see in front of your face. Or possibly it is like a cloud in the sky that goes relatively unnoticed, but blocks the sun's rays all the same.

Grief is a shape-shifter. It rarely gives you the exact same look for too long. Like a cloud when you examine it closely, it defies description. Have you ever looked very closely at a cloud in the sky? If you focus on a small segment, you will notice that it is constantly changing, moving from one shape to another. When viewed in its entirety the cloud seems to be solid and constant, but with a little scrutiny it becomes clear that this is an illusion. Grief is the same way. The large picture of our grief is that it is constant, but when viewed up close, we can get a glimpse of its mutability.

Grief is an elusive beast that demands our attention in tracking its path, and its elusiveness seems to increase as our pain recedes. This waning of grief can bring up special problems of its own, including not knowing when we have "grieved enough." There are various ways to bring conscious shape to our grief, one of which is to be aware of our increasing joy—like my joy with the music— and let that indirectly tell us about our grief. My own experience with Luke and the model rocket taught me a bit about this path of understanding. In the meantime, I continue to put energy into watching my grief recede, knowing that as surely as the tide goes out, it will just as surely come back in.

References

1. Adapted from: Gersie, Alida. *Storymaking in Bereavement.* London. 1991, Jessica Kingsley Publishers. p.151-156.
2. Moore, Robert. "Contemporary Psychotherapy as Ritual Process: an Initial Reconnaissance." *Zygon: Journal of Religion and Science.* 1983, 18:283-94.
3. "When Grief Comes Home To The Counselor." *Washington Post*, 2-22-94. p. B6.
4. Hamman, Brad. "Counting Time, About Pain and Grief and Letting Go." *Runner's World*, Nov. 1992, V. 27, no. 11, p. 102.
5. Adapted from: Gersie, Alida. p. 267.
6. Sanford, John. *The Invisible Partners.* New York, 1980, Paulist Press.
7. Rosenblatt, P.C., R.P. Walsh, and D.A. Jackson. *Grief and Mourning in Cross-Cultural Perspective.* 1976, H.R.A.F. Press.
8. Rosenblatt.
9. Some, Malidoma Patrice. *Ritual: Power, Healing and Community.* Portland. 1993, Swan Raven and Company.
10. Twitty, Anne. *Parabola.* Fall 1986.
11. Cook, J. "Dad's Double Binds, Rethinking Father's Bereavement from a Men's Studies Perspective." *The Journal of Contemporary Ethnography*, Vol. 17, No. 3, Oct. 1988, p. 285-308.
12. Counts, David. *Coping with the Final Tragedy.* 1991, Baywood Publishing.
13. Trungpa, Chogyam. *The Myth of Freedom.* 1976, Shambala.
14. Moore, Robert. *King, Warrior, Magician, Lover.* New York. 1990, Harper San Francisco.
15. Tannen, Deborah. *You Just Don't Understand.* New York. 1990, Morrow.
16. Frey, William H. *Crying: The Mystery of Tears.* 1985, Winston Press.
17. Gorman, Christine. "Sizing up the Sexes." *Time Magazine.* 1-20-92, p. 42-51.
18. Tanenbaum, Joe. *Male and Female Realities.* 1990, R. Erdmann Publishing.
19. Hoff, Bert H. "A Ritual for my Father." *M.E.N. Magazine*, March, 1993.
20. Johnson, Robert. *Inner Work.* 1986, Harper and Rowe.

References

21. Aries, Philippe. *Western Attitudes Toward Death: From the Middle Ages to the Present.* Baltimore. 1974, Johns Hopkins University Press.
22. Coffin, Margaret. *Death in Early America: The History and Folklore of Customs and Superstitions of Early Medicine, Funerals, Burials and Mourning.* Nashville. 1976, Nelson.
23. Steinfels, Peter. *Death Inside Out.* New York. 1975, Harper and Rowe. p. 25-42.
24. Rosenblatt.
25. Diallo, Yaya, and Mitchell Hall. *The Healing Drum: African Wisdom Teachings.* Rochester, Vermont. 1989, Destiny Books.
26. Reed, Janice "A Time to Live a Time to Grieve: Patterns and Processes of Mourning Among the Yolngu of Australia." *Culture, Medicine, and Psychiatry*, 3, 1979.
27. Rosenblatt.
28. Some, Malidoma. *Ritual: Power, Healing and Community.* Portland. 1993, Swan Raven and Company.

Index

Index

Index

Index

Index

Notes

Notes

Notes

ORDERING

Additional copies of *Swallowed by a Snake* can be ordered by telephone with your Mastercard or Visa by calling 1-888-870-1785 (toll-free orders only).

or in the continental U.S. by sending a check/money order for $16.95 ($13.95+$3.00 shipping) made out to "Golden Healing" and mailed to:

Golden Healing Publishing, L.L.C.
149 Little Quarry Mews
Gaithersburg, MD 20878
301-670-1027

ABOUT THE AUTHOR

Thomas Golden, LCSW is well-known in the field of healing from loss. *Swallowed by a Snake: The Gift of the Masculine Side of Healing* has been acclaimed by Elisabeth Kubler-Ross and others. Tom enjoys presenting workshops in the United States, Canada, and Australia, having been named the "1999 International Grief Educator" by the Australian Centre for Grief Education. Drawing on twenty-five years of practical, hands-on clinical experience, Tom brings a gentle sense of humor and a gift for storytelling to both his workshops and writing. His work and his web site <www.webhealing.com> have been featured in the New York Times, the Washington Post, and U.S. News and World Report, as well as on CNN and CBS Evening News.

INTERNET

You can find Tom on the World Wide Web at his award winning web site "Crisis, Grief, and Healing" at:

www.webhealing.com

Some of Tom's grief workshops are available online at his new web site:

www.griefceu.com